BY THE AUTO EDITORS OF CONSUMER GUIDE®

CONVERTIBLES

America's Dazzling Drop-Tops

PUBLICATIONS INTERNATIONAL, LTD.

The editors would like to thank the following people for supplying the photography that made this book possible:

Scott Baxter: 60
Joe Bohovic: 43, 63
Terry Boyce: 55
Thomas Glatch: 37, 41, 45, 47, 72
Eddie Goldberger: 16, 30, 32
Sam Griffith: 19, 21, 32, 33, 38, 39, 41, 42, 43, 48, 50-51, 53, 54, 55, 56, 57, 58, 63, 64, 74, 76, 90, 91
Jerry Heasley: 45
S. Scott Hutchinson: 54
Bud Juneau: 6, 10, 18, 21, 26, 28, 33, 36, 38, 39, 40, 43, 48, 52, 56, 57, 58, 62, 63, 65, 66-67, 70, 71
Milton Gene Kieft: 7, 12, 14, 15, 17, 23, 31, 32, 36, 40, 44, 45, 49, 61
Dan Lyons: 12, 32,.34, 35, 39, 41, 45, 53, 61
Vince Manocchi: cover, 11, 12, 13, 14, 15, 16, 17, 19, 20, 23, 24-25, 27, 28, 29, 31, 33, 37, 38, 41, 43, 45, 46, 47, 48, 49, 52, 54, 62, 75
Doug Mitchel: 8-9, 11, 12, 15, 16, 22, 26, 27, 30, 31, 32, 33, 37, 38, 39, 41, 42, 43, 47, 52, 53, 54, 55, 57, 58, 59, 61, 62, 64, 68, 70, 73, 76
Mike Mueller: 22, 26, 38, 39, 47, 48, 55, 65
Jay Peck: 46
William J. Schintz: 39
Richard Spiegelman: 12, 18
Steve Statham: 38
Jim Thompson: 27, 28, 69
Ken Winter: 61
Nicky Wright: 14, 15, 16, 17, 26, 27, 29, 30, 31, 36, 40, 41, 45, 46, 48, 49, 52, 54, 56, 58, 60, 61, 68, 69, 70, 73, 74, 76, 77

Contents

INTRODUCTION
ALLURE AND ORIGINS

It's no secret that the practicality of convertibles is questionable at best—but then, who purchases a convertible for practical reasons? And it's no secret, either, that throughout their history convertibles have barely made a dent in overall year-to-year production figures. Some convertible numbers may seem substantial (sales peaked at over 500,000 units in 1965), but ragtops rarely garnered more than a five percent share of the market. So why do convertibles live on?

The answer is that the American convertible is more than a car: It's a way of life, for no other body style combines the pleasures of luxury and open-air motoring. After a brief extinction in the 1970s, convertibles blossomed again on the U.S. market in the early Eighties. Barring a period as grim as the industry experienced in the late Seventies, the body style stands to remain a permanent part of the American scene.

Why? Obviously because the convertible is the *ne plus ultra* of cars as we know them—by a country mile the most desirable body style of all. A big part of that appeal is that it's often the top of the line and thus (except for limousines) a given manufacturer's costliest and cushiest model.

But beyond these objective reasons lies the very simple and emotionally powerful fact that the convertible is simply more fun than other cars. *So* much fun that convertible fans tend to forget that for about 300 days a year their cars cannot be enjoyed to the fullest unless they happen to live in the sun belt—or are slightly masochistic.

There's not much argument that, to be defined as a convertible, the car must have a top that is permanently attached to a framework that you fold down—either by hand or with a power assist—rather than remove completely (as you do the top of an MG sports car, for instance). Stricter pedants add that a convertible must have roll-up windows as well. The two-door convertible style was first referred to as a "cabriolet," later a "convertible coupe." Most four-door styles have been called "convertible sedans."

Perhaps the simplest definition is that a convertible is a car that converts from fully open to fully closed via a mechanism permanently affixed to it. And the converting part need not always be soft, as Ford proved with its famous late-Fifties "retractables." And contrary to what some purists insist, pillarless construction is not a must.

The definition must also include like-equipped two-seaters, though these have often been called "roadsters," even after their makers had given them convertible features. Of course, an open two-seater isn't automatically a roadster. By our definition, the 1955-57 Thunderbird and open Corvettes after 1955 are genuine convertibles, too.

Just when did convertibles begin? Careful reviews of body offerings indicate that they arrived in model-year 1927. And contrary to earlier accounts, they were built by far more than two or three companies. Research discloses convertibles (or "cabriolets") in the 1927 lines of no fewer than eight manufacturers: Buick, Cadillac/LaSalle, Chrysler, duPont, Lincoln, Stearns, Whippet, and Willys.

The following year brought numerous "me-too" convertibles from other manufacturers: Auburn, Franklin, Graham, Nash, Peerless, Studebaker, and Packard. Auburn and Packard were especially successful in the nascent convertible market, positioning their offerings as sophisticated luxury cars.

In 1929 Dodge, Hupmobile, and Pontiac/Oakland joined the fray. But the most important new player in 1929 was Ford, which sold 16,421 of its 2/4-passenger cabriolets during the calendar year. That was good enough to top the combined sales of all other new 1929 convertibles.

Up to this point, roadsters, touring cars, and phaetons had continued to take the lion's share of open-car sales, mainly because most every maker still had them, whereas only a few had thus far offered convertibles. But the lion's

The earliest true convertibles can be traced to 1927, when eight manufacturers, including Cadillac/LaSalle, offered them. The 2/4-passenger LaSalle cabriolet seen here is a 1928 model.

4

LaSalle (*top*) was introduced as the "junior" Cadillac in 1927. The Murphy coachbuilding firm supplied bodies for the 1928 Hudson (*above*). Lincoln's 1930 Model 188 Convertible Coupe (*right*) was at once elegant and sporting. It presaged not just a key aspect of the Lincoln allure in the 1930s and beyond, but the direction to be taken by convertibles in general. The special magic of ragtop appeal was already making itself known.

Another Murphy-bodied job was the 1928 Duesenberg Convertible Coupe, surely one of the most elegant of all drop-tops.

share wasn't what it had been. Ten years before, open cars took 90 percent of the total U.S. market; by 1929 they were at 10 percent. After 1930 their typical share was 3 percent or less, where it would remain through mid-decade; by that time, most of Detroit had simply given up on the old styles.

The reason for that, of course, is that the convertible idea took hold. Though the process was gradual to be sure, it brought a merciless thinning in the ranks of other open styles. Signs of change were apparent as early as 1932, the last year when roadsters/tourings outsold convertibles. By 1939 they accounted for only 0.3 percent of the market, whereas convertibles owned 10 times that much.

Still, the convertible had an uphill battle. It had barely come of age when the Depression, America's greatest economic catastrophe, set in. Although 17 nameplates listed convertibles for model-year 1930, this relatively expensive and luxurious body style seemed out of place in a vastly diminished market. Economic necessity soon forced the more marginal manufacturers to drop convertibles as

quickly as they'd embraced them. By decade's end, many of those companies were themselves gone for good.

The convertible survived, however, defying logic and the economic odds. The reasons it did—and some of its most splendid manifestations—are the subjects of this book.

Our purpose is to provide a general survey of American convertibles by decade. The text provides pertinent facts on the design, engineering, performance, and other traits of a model or series, primarily as they relate to the convertible versions, of course.

For brevity and to avoid duplication, this book does *not* attempt detailed descriptions of individual models. Readers seeking such information are referred to other works by the Auto Editors of Consumer Guide®: *Encyclopedia of American Cars From 1930* and *New Complete Book of Collectible Cars 1930-90*. Both of these volumes cover convertibles as well as their contemporary linemates.

7

Chapter 1: 1930-1939
Gold Amidst the Gloom

The 1930s brought a plethora of convertibles from many makers. Few were nicer than this '36 Hudson Eight.

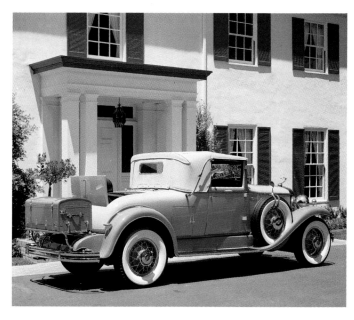

The magic that was Auburn, Cord, and Duesenberg—especially the sense of elegance (and the extravagance) that distinguished their patron, Errett Lobban Cord—brought convertibles from these marques quite early. Auburn, the humblest of the three, had been among the first practitioners of the convertible art, in 1928. A year later, soft tops were among the first Cords, the rakish L-29s.

E. L. Cord was to the Twenties what Lee Iacocca was to the Eighties. Having made his mark as a super salesman at the Moon agency in Chicago, he became president of ailing Auburn in 1926 at the age of 32. Against all odds, he soon had Auburn back on its feet. By 1930, with visions of rivaling GM and Ford, he'd added Duesenberg, engine-maker Lycoming, two coachbuilders, and several other supplier companies to his budding empire.

The *crème de la crème* among open Auburns in this period, Gordon Buehrig's famous 1935-36 Speedster, is beyond our scope, but 2/4-passenger convertible cabriolets were listed in all series from 1931. Today they're hardly less scarce than Speedsters. Full model breakouts aren't available, but Auburn's total volume plunged from over 36,000 in 1931 to just 5500 registrations by '34. That means some pretty rare individual models, convertibles especially—true gold amidst the gloom of this failed marque.

The Cord L-29 is equally rare and sought after, though it's doubtful there are any left to find. E. L. created it to fill the yawning price chasm between Auburn and the exotic Duesenberg; to assure good sales, he decreed an ultra-low stance for sensational looks. Indy race-car designer Harry Miller made that possible with his pioneering front-wheel-drive system, adapted for production by Cornelius van Ranst. Alan Leamy came up with truly classic lines of majestic proportions. The L-29 was stunning in any form, but the 2/4-passenger cabriolet and 5-seat phaeton sedan were naturally the most spectacular.

Alas, size means weight. With only a 115-horsepower Auburn straight eight to motivate it, the heavy (and *tail-heavy*) L-29 was none too good at climbing hills—or running fast on the flat. It wasn't cheap either, though prices were reduced after the 1929 debut to perk up sales. By

1931 the cabriolet was down from $3295 to $2495, the phaeton to $2595. But sales didn't perk up and production was halted in late '31 at about the 5000 mark (all bodies). The Cord wasn't finished, though; we'll return to it later.

A-C-D appropriately shunned "factory" bodies for the Duesenberg Model J, offering custom styles exclusively from the mighty car's 1928 announcement. As most every enthusiast knows, they were truly magnificent. Rollston (later Rollson) and LaGrande began offering convertible styles in 1930. Murphy, that paragon of West Coast flair, had actually built one or two convertible coupes and sedans on 1929-registered J chassis, though the majority came along in 1930-32.

There was nothing like a Duesie regardless of body, but it was truly without peer in open form. Fred Duesenberg's brains and E. L. Cord's money produced what they and many others called with no exaggeration "the world's finest motor car." One reason: its locomotive-like 420-cubic-inch Lycoming straight eight, with twin overhead camshafts driving four valves per cylinder to produce 265 horsepower—about twice the output of the industry's previous power leader, Chrysler. Equally imposing was the J's wheelbase: no less than 142.5 inches (sometimes stretched to 153.5 inches, though not for convertibles).

Only 470 Model J chassis were completed between 1928 and 1936. Though a high proportion originally carried convertible bodies, there are more soft top models now because of blatant body switching. Predictably, the company never made money with this formidable and formidably expensive masterpiece.

At the other end of the scale, the convertible began figuring into the dogfight between Ford and Chevrolet for the title of "USA 1." With the introduction of the Model A in 1928, Ford had wrested the sales lead from Bill Knudsen's surging Chevy, only to lose it again in 1931. Not until the advent of the V-8 line in 1932 would Dearborn head off Bill's car, and then only for a few years.

Offered in small numbers beginning in the A's second year, the jaunty 2/4-passenger convertible cabriolet was an established part of the Ford line by 1931. (Unlike most other body styles, however, it would be available only in standard trim through 1937, when it became a better-equipped DeLuxe.) Chevy, which had no counterpart before then, brought out a 2/4-passenger rumble-seat cabriolet in that year's new "Independence" series. At $595 and $615 respectively, both these cars were pricey, though not top of the line. Ford also built 4864 true convertible sedans, priced at $640 each; Chevy countered with 5634 two-door landau phaetons at $650 a copy.

Through mid-decade, the two-doors' sales battle mirrored the general war, with Ford triumphant; in 1934, for instance, Ford sold about 12,000 to Chevy's 3,276.

Chevrolet furloughed its cabriolet for 1935, then revived it in the restyled '36 fleet. The model continued to sell poorly, however: never more than 4000 a year. Ford did much better, and even continued convertible sedans (which Chevy never bothered with) through 1939. Dearborn's speedy V-8 was clearly preferred by soft top buyers—in retrospect, hardly surprising.

Even before the 1929 stock-market crash, the Big Two had a rival in Chrysler Corporation. Founded by Walter P. Chrysler in 1924, it soon became a "full-line" producer with the 1928 acquisition of Dodge Brothers and the introduction of Plymouth and DeSoto that same year. Well known for handsome styling in its early days, the Highland Park company had been an early advocate of convertibles. Dodge and Chrysler had them in the Twenties; Plymouth and DeSoto got them in 1930.

A hotly competitive new Plymouth appeared for 1931, still with a four-cylinder engine but outclassing its rivals with "Floating Power"—engine mounts lined with heavy rubber to insulate them from the frame. It was a simple but remarkable innovation that gave Plymouth "the smoothness of an eight and the economy of a four." Chrysler's low-price make finished third in production for the first time that year and would remain there for the next quarter-century, aided by a switch from fours to sixes effective with the '33s.

Plymouth fielded Standard and DeLuxe series from 1932, and initially issued convertibles in both. This was a shrewd departure from Ford/Chevy tactics, and it worked. While Chevy struggled to sell convertibles, Plymouth's slightly better-heeled customers took about 7000 a year in 1932-33. Then Plymouth restricted its ragtop to the DeLuxe line for 1934 and sales fell apart—curious, because the DeLuxe had previously outsold the Standard version. Successive restyles, attractive colors, and handsome leather interiors didn't seem to help. In 1937, with the industry fast recovering from the Depression, Plymouth moved only 3110 convertibles.

As an experiment, Plymouth built 690 convertible sedans for 1932, but didn't field a production model until 1939. It was only a one-year stand and just 387 were built—Chrysler Corporation's last four-door convertible. Its demise coincided with the 1940 death, at 65, of the great Walter Chrysler, who'd been ailing for several years.

DeSoto and Dodge, Chrysler's mid-range makes, offered small numbers of convertibles throughout the Thirties. (The sole exception was DeSoto's 1934 line, based on

A year before the introduction of Ford's V-8 line in 1932, Chevy outsold its rival with cars like this '31 DeLuxe sports coupe (*top*). Chrysler's 1931 "special body" convertible (*second from top*) helped propel the nameplate to the #3 spot in industry production. Only 700 of Chrysler's CD ragtops (*third from top and above*) were produced for '31.

Clockwise from top left: 1932 Auburn 8-100A; '32 Chevy DeLuxe; '32 DeSoto convertible coupe; '32 Stutz Super Bearcat; 1932 Studebaker President roadster; '32 LaSalle; '32 Ford Model B cabriolet. As the Depression deepened, Ford and Chevy fought it out for industry dominance with cars aimed at the mass buying audience. But for makes like Auburn and Stutz, which depended on the diminishing ranks of well-heeled buyers, the path was thorny; indeed, both marques disappeared after 1936.

Proud beauty: Cadillac's 1933 Victoria convertible tipped the scales at nearly three tons. Good thing the car was powered by Caddy's mammoth 452-cid 165-bhp "sweet sixteen."

the advanced but short-lived Airflow design, which was not conceived with a droptop in mind.) DeSoto's open models were among the dullest around—if that's possible—though they cost close to $1000 and came in the more deluxe of the two series. With its 1936 restyle, DeSoto attempted a convertible sedan that cost well over $1000 and thus sold only by the baker's dozen: 215 that year, 426 the next, and just 88 in 1938, after which it was dropped. Perhaps as a result, DeSoto opted out of the soft top business for 1939, then returned permanently with a convertible coupe in the handsome Ray Dietrich-styled 1940 line.

Dodge offered far more ragtops. In 1933, for example, it had no fewer than four, including a convertible sedan, all with a choice of six or eight cylinders. But the threadbare Thirties market demanded only about 1600 of them— hardly profitable. Accordingly, the division dropped its straight-eight lines for '34, built diminishing numbers of convertible sedans (none after 1938) and, like DeSoto, forgot soft tops entirely for 1939 (which probably accounts for that year's Plymouth convertible sedan).

Long overlooked among Classic-era convertibles are the singular Chryslers of 1931-33. If Chryslers were handsome before, stylist Herb Weisinger made them real headturners with his unabashed copying of the Cord L-29.

Chrysler offered rumble-seat convertible coupes in each of its four series for 1931-33, and added convertible sedans with 1932's midyear "second series" lineup. (A four-door convertible also appeared in the '31 Imperial CG series, though only 25 were built.) The 1933s were mildly altered in engine and wheelbase assignments and

gained radiators tilted back a little, but their basic design remained largely intact.

A good thing too, for these were stylish cars, particularly in topless form, and smooth performers. The big straight-eight Imperials were the most impressive, of course, their long wheelbases (126-146 inches) making the most of what Weisinger had wrought. They were fully worthy of comparison with other Classics except in technical complexity and price, which ranged from just $1325 for the 1933 Imperial Eight convertible coupe to a reasonable $3500 or so for LeBaron semi-custom styles. Other coachbuilders crafted one-off or few-at-a-time styles for various Chrysler chassis in these years, including Waterhouse in America and even a few European shops (the latter tending toward the more common Six and Eight platforms).

Chrysler abandoned roadsters and phaetons after 1931. For '34, Chrysler fielded just two folding-roof models: the Six convertible coupe ($815) and Custom Six convertible sedan ($970). Like DeSoto, Chrysler bolstered Airflows for '35 with less radical Airstream models, but with eight as well as six cylinders (DeSoto was strictly sixes in this period). Convertible coupes and sedans arrived only as Eights, but the Airflow's steady decline prompted the addition of six-cylinder versions for '36.

The Airflow bowed out after 1937, the year other Chryslers were restyled with ungainly barrel-like fronts.

Top: Although this 1933 Packard is a Dietrich model, it had no connection to coachbuilder Ray Dietrich, who had left Dietrich, Inc., in 1930. *Center:* Stutz produced this racy DV32 convertible coupe for 1933. *Bottom:* Of all the independent makes, few were as successful as Hudson's companion nameplate, Terraplane. This stylish '33 Deluxe Eight convertible coupe cost just $765.

The '38 fleet brought the return of non-Airflow Imperials and Eights, but other models were only a bit less awkward than they'd been the previous year. Much smoother lines marked the all-new '39s—but there were no convertibles, Chrysler emphasizing coupes and sedans with fancy trim and, for the Hayes-bodied victoria, distinctive rooflines. But the absence was only temporary, and convertible coupes would return for 1940.

For all the convertible activity during the Thirties, the body style was clearly on the wane by mid-decade. Sales were down, but manufacturers retained them because of the luster they lent to workaday models in showrooms. In the midst of hard times, a convertible became a symbol of something to live for.

General Motors, grounded for a decade on Alfred Sloan's marketing dictum of "a car for every purse and pocketbook" and thus the master at parting consumers from their money, continued to offer more convertibles than most anyone else, and more variety within each of its makes. The glamorous convertible sedan (which GM usually called "convertible phaeton") was another of the firm's stocks-in-trade (except at Chevrolet).

Cadillac and LaSalle, GM's top-line makes, had been among the first with true convertibles in the late Twenties. Cadillac's fabulous Sixteens and Twelves were offered with a vast array of factory and custom bodies, including convertibles as a matter of course. There was always a convertible coupe in Cadillac's "basic" eight-cylinder line, usually priced competitively. The 1933 edition, for example, cost $2845, just $50 above the relatively spartan roadster—though both represented a good year's pay for the average worker.

But it's the big multi-cylinder Cadillacs that everyone remembers, perhaps because these models were relatively uncommon after 1930-31, when they sold about 9000 units combined. Staggeringly expensive, they seemed almost vulgar in an era of widespread misery. (Other big luxury cars were shunned for the same reason. Even many of those who bought them often drove around in something less pretentious). Later, their engines were outmoded by advancing technology. For example, the introduction of precision-insert conrod bearings helped eliminate the knock and high-speed engine wear that originally enticed wealthy types away from eights. Cadillac's Twelve thus vanished after 1937; the Sixteen somehow managed to hang on through 1940.

Nineteen thirty-four brought a deftly restyled Cadillac and a new LaSalle. The latter, born in 1927 as a junior Caddy with a smaller V-8, now became a sort of glorified Buick: cut $1000 in price, given an Oldsmobile L-head straight eight and, to its credit, GM's new "Knee-Action" independent front suspension. At least it looked somewhat like the smoother, more modern new Caddy. The LaSalle two-passenger convertible coupe, a glorious expression of money-talks class consciousness in 1933, had sold for about $3000 over the previous few years. The 2/4-passenger convertible of 1934 sold for $1695, same as the four-door sedan (suggesting GM purposely took a loss on it). Better still, it weighed 700 pounds less, to the benefit of performance.

LaSalle retained convertible coupes for the rest of the decade. Convertible sedans were also available from 1937,

Clockwise from top left: 1934 Auburn; 1934 Ford roadster; '34 Packard Dietrich sedan convertible; '34 Packard V-12; '34 Packard LeBaron phaeton; 1934 Dodge Deluxe Six convertible coupe; '34 Ford V-8 convertible coupe. By the 1934 model year, open cars of all types accounted for about three percent of the auto market; just two years later, that figure had shrunk to one percent.

15

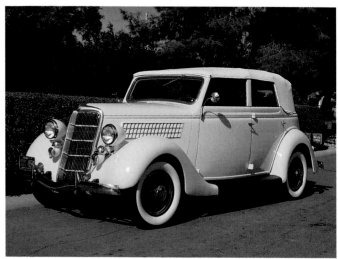

Buick's 1935 68C convertible (*top left*) offered 100 horsepower for $1675, but because the convertible sedan style was fading in popularity, only 575 were built. The coupe version of the same model (*top right*) was more popular. Ford won friends with the '35 740 (*above left*); Studebaker's '35 Commander Eight (*above right*) sold for about $1000.

when Cadillac power returned. Prices were cut further in later years to encourage sales. The soft top was down to $1255 by 1936, a long way from the heady sums of 1927-33. But Cadillac's medium-price Depression-fighter was a terminal case, being slowly squeezed out of its market by Buick as the economy inched toward recovery. Thus, only 855 two-door and 265 four-door convertibles were built for 1938; the respective 1939 figures were 1056 and 185. LaSalle's last hurrah came with the 1940 models, again adroitly styled by GM's Harley Earl. In some ways, they were the best LaSalles since the first ones.

Buick, Olds, and Pontiac fared better than LaSalle, both generally and with convertibles. Buick was GM's convertible king, largely because it covered the widest market in the company. By 1931 the division was established with a four-series lineup (50, 60, 80, and 90) costing $1000-$2000, which was quite a span in those days. Two years later it had a convertible in each line except the Series 90, which got one for '34. With the '36s came the now-familiar Special, Century, Roadmaster, and Limited names. By that point, Buick usually offered five or six convertibles a year, including four-door "phaetons" in the two senior series, plus Special and Century versions in 1937-38.

For most of the decade, Buick's annual soft top production was 1500-3500 units, the majority being Special and Century convertible coupes. Phaetons were discarded

after 1938 and saw far fewer copies: that year just 946 Specials, 219 Centurys, and 411 Roadmasters.

Oldsmobile and Pontiac, with narrower market assignments and considerably trimmed lineups after 1933, built fewer soft tops in this period. Nevertheless, Olds fielded at least one convertible in each series each year save 1934, when an eight-cylinder model was its lone entry. Pontiac offered but a single six-cylinder series in 1931, added a V-8 line for '32 (an extension of recently deceased Oakland), then went to straight eights for 1933-34. Each of these contained a convertible. Pontiac then blossomed into two Sixes and an Eight for 1935-36, each with a version of what it called a 2/4-passenger cabriolet.

In strict Sloan fashion, Pontiac convertibles usually sold for $800-$900, Oldsmobiles for about $900-$1100, this at a time when $100-$200 was a big difference. We should also not forget that Oakland, Pontiac's parent, had a convertible in its swan-song '31 line, priced at $995.

Unlike Buick, Pontiac and Olds bothered with convertible sedans only from time to time: Pontiac in 1937-38,

Olds in the big 98 series of 1940-41. The latter was impressive on its 125-inch wheelbase and cost the world for an Oldsmobile: about $1600. This may explain why production ran to only 50 units in the first year and 119 in the second.

The big guns among Thirties independents were Hudson (helped immeasurably by its offshoot Essex and Terraplane makes), Studebaker (when not in receivership), and Packard (after 1935, when it became a volume manufacturer by dint of the successful, lower-priced One Twenty). Hudson had popularized the closed coach as an Essex model in the Twenties, but stuck with the traditional roadster and touring until 1932, when it finally switched to convertibles for both Hudson and Essex.

The big Hudson changed as dramatically as LaSalle once the Depression set in. Volume plummeted from a rollicking 300,000 units in 1929 to barely 40,000 four years later.

Hudson limited itself to a single convertible in 1932-33, then listed one or more in most series. By 1938, convertible coupes and broughams were offered in a reabsorbed Terraplane line (DeLuxe and Super models) as well as in the senior 112, Custom Six, and Deluxe Eight series. All were two-doors. Convertible coupes had a single bench seat for three; broughams were conventional six-seaters.

The low-price Essex had helped Hudson rise as high as third in the industry in 1927, but couldn't sustain itself after the Great Crash. What kept Hudson going was the smart and speedy Terraplane, an Essex offering in 1932-33, a separate make in 1934-37, a Hudson series in 1938 (after which the name was discarded). Terraplanes would generally do up to 80 mph and 25 miles per gallon yet cost as little as $425; convertibles were priced almost $200 higher, though. Adding to its appeal was an extra-cost eight-cylinder evolution of the original Essex Six, offered beginning in 1933.

The first Essex convertibles, Pacemaker and Terraplane, arrived for 1932. All Essex models were called Terraplane the following year, when a convertible was cataloged in each of the line's five series. Models were then cut and the Eight dropped as Essex disappeared and Terraplane became a separate make. However, there were usually two convertible coupes each year and, in 1937, convertible broughams, too. Of course, the open cars sold for much more than the average Terraplane: $725-$845 in 1937, for example, when closed cars started at $595. But their numbers and variety reflected well on the Terraplane's sporty and youthful personality.

At Studebaker, the failures of the Erskine and Rockne, plus the purchase of Pierce-Arrow, meant hard economic times and a concentration on volume models; with one exception, Studebaker would build nothing but closed cars through 1946.

But that exception was a dandy: a convertible sedan in the 1938-39 Commander and President series. Big and impressive, it sold for a whopping $300-$350 more than the next costliest model in each line. The predictable results were meager sales and very low production, making these some of the rarest and most desirable prewar Studeys for today's collectors.

Studebaker's future partner, Packard, probably experienced the greatest image change of any independent in

The 1936 Chevrolet cabriolet (*top*) marked Chevy's return to that body style after a one-year layoff. A cabriolet of another sort altogether was Cord's awe-inspiring 1936 810 (*second from top*); note the hidden headlamps. Ford's Deluxe cabriolet (*third from top*) was a popular item for 1936, with production of 14,068. The snappy Packard One Twenty (*above*) represented the bottom of Packard's line for 1936.

the Thirties. From a maker of luxury cars "for a discriminating clientele," Packard moved gingerly downmarket with the Light Eight of 1932, then aggressively with the One Twenty of 1935 and the Six of 1937. These do-or-die medium-price models not only saved the company's hide but made Packard a significant contender in the annual production race for the first time. From its accustomed 18th place and an almost negligible 4803 units in 1933, Packard leaped to a strong eighth and a record 123,000 cars by 1937. The One Twenty ("Eight" in 1938), accompanied by the Packard Six after 1936, accounted for well over 90 percent of production. Both were offered as convertible coupes, and the One Twenty was also available as a convertible sedan.

Packard naturally offered convertible coupes on its senior Eight and Twelve chassis throughout the decade, though they were a very small percentage of a total volume that itself was small. Record 1937, for example, produced 115,500 Sixes and One Twentys against 5793 Super Eights and 1300 Twelves. The grand old Twelve, once queen of the line and a standard for America, vanished after model-year 1939 and only 446 assemblies.

Among the smaller independents, Willys built no convertibles after 1930. Hupmobile released its first convert-

The aptly named 1937 Cord Sportsman (*above left*) offered "coffin-nose" styling at its most aggressive. At $1350, the '37 LaSalle convertible coupe (*above right*) was positioned to rival Packard's One Twenty. Despite their limited audience, convertible sedans continued, as witness this '37 DeSoto Six (*below*).

ibles in 1929 and generally had one in each series each year, variously calling it convertible coupe, convertible cabriolet, and roadster cabriolet. Hupp's last convertibles appeared in conventionally styled six- and eight-cylinder series for 1934. The firm took a hiatus in mid-1936, reopened fitfully in 1937-38, then closed for good.

Graham, whose history parallels Hupp's, dropped all its soft top models after 1937. This automaker also had its best year before the Depression, then entered the Thirties with too many models for the shrunken market: sixes and eights in five series. Sales were down to 20,000 by 1931, then dropped by half over the next two years.

Graham produced its best convertibles in its leanest years. Notable is the Blue Streak Eight of 1932, beautifully sculpted by Amos Northup, creator of the '31 Reo Royale. The Blue Streak's skirted fenders prefigured an industry trend, and its 245-cid straight eight boasted an advanced aluminum cylinder head. The convertible, a 2/4-seater, came only in DeLuxe trim for 1932; a Standard model was added for 1933-34 along with six-cylinder running mates.

For 1935, Graham unleashed the Super-charged Custom Eight, America's first popular-price "hyperaspirated" car, packing 135 horsepower. Over the next six years, Graham would build more blown production cars than anyone else before, but it wasn't enough to ensure a happy future. The 1936 line comprised sixes only, normal and supercharged, including standard and Custom Supercharger convertibles. These continued through 1937, after which Graham abandoned soft tops and pinned its hopes—in vain, as it turned out—on the odd "Spirit of Motion" design now widely known as the "Sharknose."

Mention of the last Hupps and Grahams inevitably leads us to the second and final Cord, the great 810/812 of 1936-37. Bodies for the abortive rear-drive Hupp Skylark/Graham Hollywood of 1940-41 were made using dies obtained after Cord Corporation's collapse, but all were sedans; the 810/812 convertibles weren't similarly reincarnated (except for a prototype Skylark).

Like its L-29 predecessor, the 810 employed front-wheel drive but was far more compact and maneuverable, thanks to a Lycoming V-8 with 115 bhp. The 1937-model 812 was little changed apart from optional availability of a Schwitzer-Cummins supercharger that boosted power to 170, and an astounding 190 with the "high-boost" package. So equipped, an 812 would do nearly 110 mph and 0-60 mph in 13 seconds, which made it among the fastest of prewar American cars.

There were two 810/812 convertibles, both two-doors: the aptly named Sportsman, a two-seat cabriolet, and a four-passenger four-window "convertible sedan" called Phaeton. They were relative bargains, too, at about $2600. Alas, production delays and mechanical woes doomed Cord's comeback, and relatively few 810/812s were sold.

Nash survived these difficult years by merging with the Kelvinator appliance firm in 1937, which brought a bonus in the person of Kelvinator's cigar-chomping president, George Mason. Early-Thirties Nashes were sumptuous, beautifully styled cars with many special features. Notable was "Twin Ignition," meaning two sets of spark plugs/points/condensers/coils operating from a single distributor; overhead valves, an idea Charlie Nash probably got when he managed Buick; and nine main bearings for all straight eights. Styling was classically upright through 1933. A more streamlined group of '34s previewed 1935's still-swoopier "Aero-form" design with rounded lines and pontoon fenders. Successive facelifts belied its promise, however, and Nashes weren't really pretty again until 1939, appearing with flush-fit headlights and a slim vertical prow.

Through 1934, Nash soft tops were conventional rumble-seat cabriolets and convertible sedans. Convertibles vanished with the '35 restyle (and a drastic, Depression-inspired model cutback), but an appropriately smooth 3/5-passenger cabriolet joined the '37 line, offered as a

Pontiac's 1937 Deluxe Eight convertible sedan (*top right and second from top*) sold for $1235; six-cylinder models went for $1197. The mighty '37 Packard Twelve convertible coupe (*third from top*) ran with a 175-bhp V-12—plenty of power for this 5255-pound beauty. Olds (*right*) offered two convertible coupes for 1937; one with a six, and the other, seen here, with an eight.

The nation remained in the grip of the Depression in 1938. No surprise, then, that Cadillac's Series 90 convertible sedan (*top*)—priced at a mind-boggling $6000—found only 13 buyers. At once imposing and sporting, the 5350-pound 90 was powered by a 185-bhp V-16. Lincoln wasn't exactly snoozing during the '38 model year, as witness the V-12 Zephyr (*above, left and right*); 600 of them were sold for $1700 each. More economical still was Nash's 1938 Ambassador Six convertible cabriolet (*right*), which went for $1099.

low-price Lafayette 400 and as a plush Ambassador Six and Eight.

Announced in the improving economic climate of 1939 was a new Ford make that's still with us: Mercury, named for the speedy "messenger of the gods." The brainchild of company president Edsel Ford, it was Dearborn's first direct competitor to GM's B-O-P trio and the Dodge/DeSoto duo from Chrysler. Compared to that year's Ford, the first Merc was just a little larger, more powerful, and accordingly more expensive, and ad writers waxed poetic over its column-mounted gearlever. But it was a good seller. The market called for about 75,000 of the '39s, divided among three sedans and a five-seat "convertible club coupe," a $1018 top-liner. Mercury volume would continue at this level through 1941.

Like main rivals Packard and Cadillac, Ford's luxury leader, Lincoln, cataloged a plethora of factory and custom bodies for its big L, K, KA, and KB chassis of 1930-35. This naturally included convertible coupes and sedans, mainly supplied by the likes of Brunn, Dietrich, and LeBaron. All were predictably scarce: In 1934, for example, just 25 Brunns, 45 LeBarons, and 25 Dietrichs were manufactured. As with Cadillac's Sixteen, the lush Lincoln K and its big V-12 would be built through 1940 in rapidly diminishing numbers, which made for individual open models as rare as any in this period.

Again like its rivals, Lincoln weathered hard times by fleeing to the medium-price field, but with a far more radical car: the 1936 Zephyr. Based on a rear-engine concept by John Tjaarda, it emerged with a conventional chassis and the most balanced streamlining yet seen from Detroit—a tribute to Edsel Ford and E. T. "Bob" Gregorie. It was also the first car in which aircraft-type stress analysis actually proved the advantage of unit construction. The Zephyr's powerplant, a 100-bhp L-head V-12 derived from Ford's flathead V-8, proved troublesome, but sales took off as Lincoln, like Packard, became a high-volume make for the first time in its history.

Zephyr body styles initially comprised the expected coupe and sedan. Convertibles didn't appear until 1938, but they were worth the wait: two- and four-door models that benefited from that year's effective facelift and longer wheelbase. The basically similar '39s were further improved via hydraulic brakes (belatedly adopted across the board in Dearborn) and a cooler-running V-12. Though worthy collectibles in their own right, these open Zephyrs led to an even more coveted convertible: the gorgeous first-generation Continental, not in production until 1940, though the prototype built for Edsel Ford was based on a '39 Zephyr.

Less happy fates awaited one-time Lincoln foes Franklin and Pierce-Arrow, as well as Reo, a producer of excellent cars with singular styling. All went under well before the Forties dawned, not for lack of merit but as victims of the era's harsh economic realities.

Franklin chassis were the basis for many custom bodies. One of the more unusual was the Pirate, a four-door convertible designed by Ray Dietrich, with concave lower-body contours that fully covered the running boards—something everyone would have 10 years hence. Dietrich also built four-passenger speedsters with foreshortened bodywork. Most were closed cars with permanent canvas-

Packard fielded six-, eight-, and 12-cylinder convertibles for 1938. The Eight convertible coupe (*top two photos*) ran with 120-bhp and sold for $1365. Pontiac's 1938 Deluxe Eight cabriolet (*third from top*) offered 100 horsepower and sold for $1057. And for bargain hunters, there was Chevy's '38 Master cabriolet (*above*) for $755.

Clockwise from top left: Buick's lowest-priced drop-top for 1939 was the Series 40 convertible coupe, available for $925; Cadillac's '39 Series 61 convertible coupe came with a 135-bhp V-8 for $1770; at Ford, the 1939 model year brought the Deluxe convertible coupe (*two views*), which offered an 85-bhp V-8 for $788. Buyers apparently found the Ford's combination of price, performance, and good looks hard to resist, for 10,422 of these ragtops were produced. For the first time, Ford gearshifts were column-mounted and brakes were hydraulic.

covered tops, but a full-convertible option was available at extra cost.

A convertible coupe was included in Franklin's new 1933 Olympic series, the firm's lowest-priced model line ever, cobbled up in a vain effort to stem mounting money losses. Powered by an L-head six *sans* supercharger, it was the product of a collaboration with Reo: basically a badge-engineered version of that outfit's latest Flying Cloud. At about $1500, the Olympic convertible was a good value, well built and pretty, but it was too little too late. Olympic production barely topped 1000 units for 1933-34; convertibles amounted to fewer than 100.

At Reo, founded in 1904 by Ransom E. Olds (hence the acronym), the lineup was far too broad to sustain in the withering early-Thirties market. It was radically thinned by 1934 as the firm tried desperately to economize, though convertibles would persist for one more year. Still, the Flying Clouds, even the late shorter-wheelbase models, were truly beautiful, and the 135-inch-wheelbase Custom Eight convertible was as handsome a car as America built in these years. Reo ceased car production in September 1936, though it survived as a truckmaker for another 40 years.

Convertible sedans and roadster-coupes were offered by Pierce-Arrow, another fine marque that, in 1938, fell prey to Depression-era economics. Sales diminished steadily from 1933 to 1937, but during this period Pierce offered about as many open body styles as anyone. Among its 1934-35 Eights and 1936 models were "convertible roadster-coupes" seating just two passengers in utter glory on huge wheelbases. But production was the lowest imaginable. In 1937, for example, Pierce completed only 121 eight-cylinder cars in all, and just a handful were convertibles. That year's Twelves numbered only 71, with open styles totaling fewer than 10.

Although the convertible coupe body style had almost completely supplanted the convertible sedan as the Thirties drew to a close, there's no denying the allure (or $5828 price) of the 1939 Lincoln Model K V-12 four-door (*above left*), with body by LeBaron. Mercury bowed for 1939, and included the V-8, 95-bhp convertible club coupe (*above top*), priced at $1018. Plymouth's '39 convertible coupe (*above*) handily outsold its convertible-sedan stablemate.

Marmon, Jordan, and Peerless—all of which had offered convertibles—were other makes that died during the Depression. But ironically, the automotive design developments of 1940-1975 would be almost wholly the result of lessons learned during the Thirties. If the Depression meant the end for some companies, it forced the survivors to think, plan, and invent. In so doing, they literally altered the shape of the automobile's future. Not until the fuel crises and market upheavals of the 1970s would American cars be so dramatically transformed.

Likewise, the Thirties saw open body styles change from "regular" models to the epitome of devil-may-care playfulness. One by one in 1929-30, then with a rush in 1931-34, the major manufacturers switched from old-fashioned roadsters and tourings to genuine convertibles—coupes and sedans with convenient folding tops and roll-up glass windows. Gradually, convertible-top mechanisms acquired power assistance: hydraulic at first (as early as 1939), later electric. Meanwhile, the convertible coupe handily outgunned the costlier convertible sedan in popularity.

The Thirties, then, was the era when the convertible acquired its modern image as a car for a limited but necessary market, designed as the ultimate sporty style among production bodies. Both trends would continue in the Forties, though they'd be interrupted by war and stalled a bit afterwards by an even more practical development: the *hardtop* convertible.

23

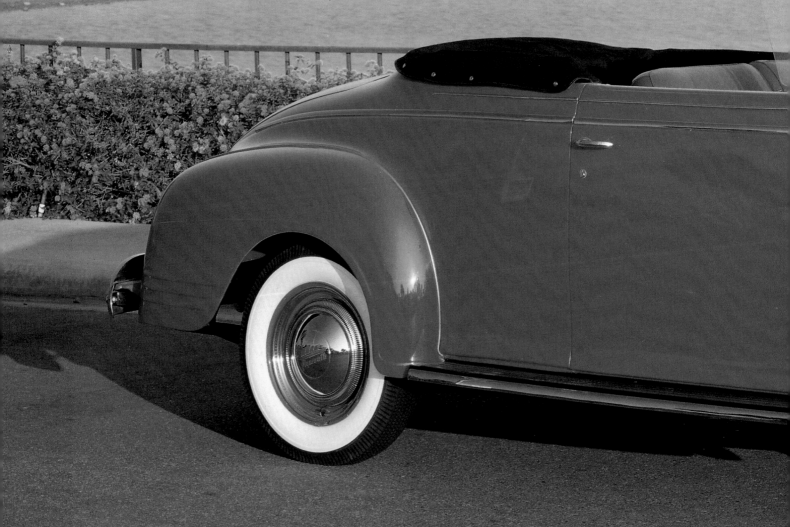

CHAPTER 2: 1940-1949
THE RACE TO PRODUCE

As the U.S. economy geared up for war work in the early 1940s, convertibles sold well. Plymouth's 1941 Special DeLuxe, priced at $1007, found 10,545 buyers.

D espite (or perhaps because of) the expanding war in Europe, Detroit produced nearly 3.3 million cars in 1940, and a record 4.3 million for 1941. But by the last day of 1941 the nation had been at war for three weeks, and civilian car production ended by government order two months later; it would not resume for nearly four years.

Before the enforced hiatus, convertibles sold well in a market swollen by the demands of a national economy revived by war work. About 160,000 were built in 1940-42—nearly 100,000 in 1941 alone, when soft tops garnered a respectable 2.7-percent market share. Industry ranks had been sadly depleted, however. Big Three aside, the only automakers still around were independents American Bantam, Graham-Paige, Hudson, Hupmobile, Nash, Packard, Studebaker, and Willys-Overland. Of these, Hupp and W-O would leave the automobile business after 1941.

American Bantam of Butler, Pennsylvania, would disappear too, but not before building its only convertible: designer Alex Tremulis's cute little Riviera, a more civilized and stylish variant of the Bantam, itself a license-built version of Britain's cheap and cheery Austin Seven. Forties Bantams were powered by a 20-horsepower, 50-cubic-inch four-cylinder engine (up from 13 bhp and 46 cid) in a simple chassis spanning a petite 75-inch wheelbase. The Riviera was the prettiest model, but Americans weren't quite ready for tiny cars of any kind. The firm was almost broke by 1939, when it built just 1229 vehicles. While turning out fewer than 1000 cars in 1940-41, Bantam sought salvation in the Army's new general-purpose-vehicle project, supplying the first acceptable prototype for what became the Jeep. It later turned entirely to building Jeeps, but the Army needed them faster than Bantam could deliver, and the firm went under once its contract was canceled.

Before proceeding further, we should note that the convertible sedan disappeared from the American scene after 1942, not to return until Kaiser-Frazer's cobbled-up afterthought of 1949. Poor sales were obviously to blame: By 1941, entire industry production was less than 2000 units.

Of the majors, only General Motors bothered with "convertible phaetons" after 1939. Buick offered one in each of its five 1940 series, then deleted all but the Super and Roadmaster versions for '41 (though special-order styles on the top-line Limited chassis were still cataloged, most executed by Brunn). Oldsmobile, meantime, belatedly fielded its first and only convertible sedans, both top-liners: a Series 90 for 1940 ($1570), and a Custom Cruiser 8 (Series 98) for '41 ($1575).

LaSalle breathed its last in 1940, the only year when Cadillac's companion make offered two model lines. These were beautiful cars and somewhat scarce, none more than the ragtops. The junior Series 50 saw just 599 convertible coupes and 125 convertible sedans; respective figures for the plusher Series 52 Special were 425 and a mere 75. Cadillac then stepped up production of its Series

Despite having a 141-bhp straight eight, Buick's 1940 Century convertible (*left, top*) found only 550 buyers. Ford's V-8-equipped 1940 DeLuxe convertible (*second from top*) could not outsell its six-cylinder Chevy counterpart. Mercury added a convertible sedan for 1940, but the same year's two-door ragtop (*third from top*) received only a minor facelift. Packard's entry-level ragtop for 1940 was the $1100 One Ten (*bottom*).

62 convertible sedan and priced it $230 below the 1940 version (of which only 75 were built). The result hardly seemed worth the effort, though: a paltry 400 for the entire 1941 model year.

America's only other late-prewar convertible sedans came from Mercury (1940) and Packard (1940-41). The 1940 Mercurys, which also included three closed sedans and a convertible coupe, were lovely, with rounded, prow-front styling by the talented Bob Gregorie. The Packards were far more opulent; those with bodies designed by Howard A. "Dutch" Darrin were possibly the most beautiful four-door convertibles ever built.

Darrin's Packard connection stemmed from his 1937 decision to return from Paris to Hollywood, where he set up a studio to create exotic adaptations of production cars for movieland society. His first such Packard was a convertible coupe on a 1938 Eight chassis for singer-actor Dick Powell; he did another 16-18 similar customs in 1938-39. With these, Dutch convinced Packard to add three Darrins to its 1940 catalog: convertible victoria (coupe), convertible sedan, and four-door sport sedan.

While Dutch had previously worked on the One Twenty chassis, Packard insisted that these "production" Darrins be Super Eights (Series One Eighty) for prestige reasons. The sport sedan was quickly dropped, so most Darrin Packards were convertible victorias. Only five '40s and one '41 were convertible sedans, but they were the best of the lot. And their prices were as stunning as their looks: around $4600 for the two-door, an imposing $6300 for the four-door.

The 1940-42 Packard lines abounded with convertible coupes and sedans, starting with the $1100 One Ten two-door. Though four-door converts were dropped after '41, two-doors were retained, as were their older, four-square bodies. The all-new '41 Clipper sedan, the first envelope-body Packard, met with great acclaim, but the war precluded a convertible derivative (though there would have been one otherwise by 1943).

Packard would get around to a Clipper-based ragtop, but not until the unfortunate "pregnant elephant" restyle of 1948. By that point, the felt lack of a convertible was so

A sextet of 1941 models. *Top row, from left:* Buick's stately Roadmaster; Chevrolet Special DeLuxe, which sold 15,296 copies; Chrysler's sedately styled Windsor. *Bottom row, from left:* DeSoto Custom, the make's only ragtop for the year; Ford Super DeLuxe, showing the "busier" front-end styling adopted for '41; and the V-12 Lincoln Zephyr. Despite the beauty and power of the Zephyr ragtop, only 725 were produced.

acute that Packard released the Super Eight version six months before the rest of the line. Despite a shortish, 120-inch wheelbase, it was an impressive-looking car for the day and relatively popular, with sales of 7763 at $3250 each. Far more lavish was that year's Custom Eight ($4295), riding the 127-inch chassis and carefully crafted inside and out. Counting 1105 Custom Eights, Packard was the largest producer of luxury convertibles that year—for the first and last time after the war. From 1949 on, Cadillac's lone soft top would outsell all of Packard's by four to one.

The only other convertibles from independent producers in 1940 were Nashes and Hudsons. All were fine examples of the two-door breed (although Hudson's 1940-42 soft tops were called "convertible sedans"), with fresh, contemporary styling.

Hudson's 1941 convertibles were engineered to be as solid and durable as its sedans (rare among period ragtops), with a specially designed, heavily reinforced frame for the first time. Hudson also offered its first power top, controlled by a dashboard button. Rear side windows were now standard but no longer detachable, lowering with the top instead. Offerings comprised DeLuxe and Super Sixes and Commodore Six and Eight (the last three on 121-inch wheelbases, versus the DeLuxe's 116). All continued for 1942.

Nash, like Hudson, had fully restyled for 1939. Its '40 facelift was similar, with a pointed nose carrying a slim vertical grille between chromed "catwalks" inboard of the headlamps. Nash switched to unit construction for 1941 but retained a separate body/chassis Ambassador convertible (called "All-Purpose cabriolet") in limited production for that year only. The model didn't surface again until 1948 when 1000 were built; these were Nash's last large ragtops.

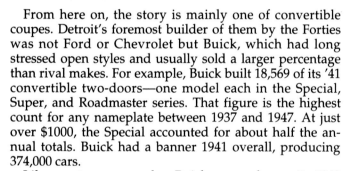

From here on, the story is mainly one of convertible coupes. Detroit's foremost builder of them by the Forties was not Ford or Chevrolet but Buick, which had long stressed open styles and usually sold a larger percentage than rival makes. For example, Buick built 18,569 of its '41 convertible two-doors—one model each in the Special, Super, and Roadmaster series. That figure is the highest count for any nameplate between 1937 and 1947. At just over $1000, the Special accounted for about half the annual totals. Buick had a banner 1941 overall, producing 374,000 cars.

Like most everyone else, Buick warmed over its 1942 models as stopgaps for the first three years after the war, but the Special convertible and Century series didn't return. Relying strictly on $2000-$3000 Super and Roadmaster two-doors, Buick continued with the industry's highest convertible volume: 8600 in 1946, 40,000 in 1947, 30,000 in 1948.

As for Cadillac, it spread down into the upper region of LaSalle's former price territory once its companion make departed. One result was that a 1941-42 Sixty-Two convertible coupe could be had for under $2000. But the ragtop didn't sell; perhaps people were not aware of the price. Only 908 went out the door during 1940-42. Postwar, it was a different story: 1342 of the '46s, 6755 of the '47s. The Sixty-Two was the only Caddy convertible to survive the war, but then it was the only one needed.

In GM's mid-price ranks, Olds and Pontiac worked hard at ragtops prewar, selling 11,000 of their '41s combined. Neither make listed fewer than two models, usually split between the top and bottom series. The Pontiacs

Top left: The gorgeous Lincoln Continental became a separate series for 1941, rather than part of the Zephyr series. *Top right:* The Custom Cruiser 8 was the top of the Olds line for '41. *Bottom left:* Packard's '41 One Twenty, priced at $1407, cost half as much as the Continental. *Bottom right:* Plymouth's 1941 Special DeLuxe, with dramatically styled parking lamps and split heart-shaped grille.

cost about $1000; the '41 Oldsmobiles ranged from a $1048 six-cylinder 66 to the $1227 eight-cylinder 98 version. Both makes fielded similar offerings postwar, albeit at higher, inflation-fueled prices. The Olds 98 became one of GM's first new postwar cars with its mid-1948 "Futuramic" redesign, but no convertibles were immediately available. The old 98 remained popular, though. It accounted for about three-fourths of the make's 1948 convertible sales, which totaled close to 17,000, making Olds number three in soft tops behind Buick and Chevy. (Pontiac, at 16,000, ranked fourth.)

Chevy's convertibles finally began outselling Ford's in 1940, when new "Royal Clipper" styling made for a thoroughly more attractive car than Chevy had built for some time. (Not inaccurately, some still describe it as a mini-Cadillac or Buick.) Chevrolet achieved this success with just one top-line convertible selling at $800-$1000 (a Special DeLuxe for 1940-41, a Fleetmaster for 1942-48) and continued its lead after the war except 1946. With its plodding "Stovebolt" six, a Chevy convertible couldn't keep pace with an open Ford V-8, but at least it looked better.

Ford and Mercury were restyled for 1941, but neither was an improvement. For the model year, Ford built only 700,000 cars while Chevy topped the million mark for the first time. The advent of an overhead-valve Ford Six

28

didn't help, though it was also offered as a convertible. Again like most others, both Dearborn makes relied on warmed-over '42s for 1946-48, but added luster to the lines with new limited-production convertibles: the pricey ($1982-$2209), wood-bodied Ford/Mercury Sportsmans.

Glamour was left to Lincoln, and model-year 1940 brought one of the decade's most stunning cars, the Zephyr-based Continental, an Edsel Ford idea executed by Bob Gregorie. Rakish long-hood/short-deck proportions, Dearborn's then-favored prow front, outside spare tire, and a sleek yet "formal" roofline made it "thoroughly continental" per Edsel's instructions. A closed coupe and wide-quarters cabriolet were offered at $2850 each, and they lured customers into dealerships by the thousands (some of whom went away in one of the less-expensive Zephyrs, which still included a shapely convertible two-door). The '41 Continental, split off from the Zephyr line, enjoyed slightly higher volume.

For 1942, all Lincolns acquired a more reliable, 305-cid version of the flathead Zephyr V-12, plus a flashy facelift with higher, squared-up fenders; reduced ride height; and chromier, more complex grillework. The last was revised for postwar models, which were prewar carryovers except that the 292-cid engine returned and the "Zephyr" name did not. The Continental reached a yearly production peak in 1947 at 1569 units, only to vanish a year later (though not permanently).

Chrysler Corporation's 1940-42 convertibles were conventional and low-key, sprinkled among the various line-ups wherever it was thought they'd do the most good. Chrysler offered Windsor Six and New Yorker Eight models, the former occasionally sporting vivid "Highlander plaid" or "Navajo" upholstery. Dodge and Plymouth had one apiece, slotted into their higher-price spreads. Ditto DeSoto except for 1942, when it offered Custom and Deluxe ragtops.

One of the most memorable of all Chryslers surfaced in 1946: the wood-trimmed Town & Country, a sleek wagon prewar, now an elegant closed sedan and convertible coupe. The last T&C ragtops of 1949 sold for $3900, which was more than most Cadillacs, while all-steel Windsor and New Yorker convertibles soldiered on at $2000-$2500. In all, more than 8500 T&Cs were built through early 1949, making it more successful than Ford's Sportsmans.

In the unprecedented seller's market of 1946, Studebaker released the industry's first new postwar soft tops: the 1947 Regal Deluxe Champion ($1902) and Commander ($2236), of which 6000 were built by January 1948. The 112-inch-wheelbase Champion was on the stubby side, but the Commander looked very good indeed, a tribute to the radical new styling by Virgil Exner of the Raymond Loewy team.

Hudson and Kaiser-Frazer built the most unorthodox early-postwar soft tops. The former debuted its famous "Step-down" cars for 1948, with smooth, low lines and unitized construction of granite-like strength. Among them were no fewer than three convertibles, more than any other manufacturer: Super Six and Commodore Six/Eight. Called "brougham" (thus reviving pre-1940 nomenclature), they bore a broad steel header above the windshield. Hudson claimed superior rollover protection, but simple economics explains the header's existence: It

From top: Buick's handsomely styled 1942 Roadmaster came with a 165-bhp straight eight; Dodge's $1245 '42 Custom convertible coupe outsold its Chevy counterpart (by three units), despite costing nearly $200 more; the '42 Lincoln Zephyr carried an enlarged 305-cid V-12 with 130 bhp.

was merely a remnant of decapitating the closed two-door body to eliminate the need for separate convertible dies.

Kaiser-Frazer's convertible, announced for 1949, was unique for its day in having four doors. Production economies were at work here, too, because a four-door sedan was all K-F had bodywise. Like Hudson's, its convertible's header was carved from a sedan roof, leaving a small but noticeable expanse of steel. Only 124 of the '49s were called for: about 66 Kaisers and 46 Frazers. A handful were reserialed as 1950 models.

Ford and Chrysler entered 1949 with all-new designs across the board, and GM completed its postwar overhaul with like updates for Chevy, Pontiac, Buick, and the junior Oldsmobiles. (The Olds 98, as mentioned, and all Cadillacs except limos were redesigned for '48.) Ford and GM adopted much sleeker lines on full-envelope bodies; Chrysler persisted with bolt-on rear fenders and a more upright stance.

Buick, once a cornucopia of convertibles, canceled its Super but produced over 30,000 Special and Roadmaster

Following a wartime hiatus, Detroit auto production resumed in 1946. DeSoto's only convertible for the year was a coupe in the Custom series (*top left*), a virtual carryover from 1942; Dodge's mildly facelifted '46 Custom convertible (*top right*) could be had for $1649; like Ford, Mercury offered a wood-sided Sportsman ragtop (*above*) for 1946.

models. These were massive, brightly decorated cars selling respectively for about $2100 and $3100 and riding 121/126-inch wheelbases. Chevy did even better with 32,932 examples of its sole convertible, in the Styleline Deluxe series, a neat little car still well liked today. Cadillac continued with its solitary Series 62 ragtop, of which 8000 were sold at $3442. Pontiac and Oldsmobile, spanning a broader price spread, offered five convertibles between them. Olds served up three, ranging from $2148 (in the six-cylinder 76 series, fast waning in sales) to $2973 (the big 98, the most popular at 12,602 units). The Pontiacs were all deluxe-trim models in the Chieftain Six and Eight series, tagged at around $2200.

But Ford had America's favorite 1949 convertible, wresting the sales lead from Chevy on the strength of its fine

Buick sold 40,371 convertibles in 1947, including this Super (*top*); Chrysler's very desirable '47 Town & Country (*middle row, left*) sported real wood paneling; Ford sold 2250 wood-sided Sportsman ragtops (*middle row, right*) in 1947, up from 1209 in 1946; Pontiac's 1947 Torpedo (*left*); Studebaker offered an all-new convertible for 1947 and advertised itself as "First by far with a postwar car"—no doubt that Studey's '47 Champion convertible (*above*) was a head-turner.

Clockwise from top left: Cadillac's befinned 1948 Sixty-Two found 5450 buyers at $3442; Lincoln's '48 Zephyr convertible was priced at $3142, but found far fewer buyers than the Caddy; the 1948 Nash Ambassador convertible coupe was Nash's first postwar ragtop; the same year brought Packard's "pregnant elephant" styling, seen here on a convertible coupe; Studebaker's Commander Regal DeLuxe, priced at $2431, was the most expensive Study for 1948; Lincoln ended the Continental Mark I series with the imposing '48 models.

new postwar design by Dick Caleal of the George Walker organization. Offered only as a Custom V-8, the soft top accounted for 51,133 units, the highest of any Ford convertible yet. Lincoln and Mercury were also rebodied for '49, becoming large, bulbous "bathtub" styles—distinctive if not exactly pretty (though arguably more so than Nash's similar attempt). Lincoln had two soft tops, standard and Cosmopolitan, costing $3200/$4000 and produced sparingly: only 743 for the calendar year. Mercury's single entry, priced at a more attractive $2416, brought 16,765 sales, another record.

At Chrysler in 1949, Plymouth, Dodge, and DeSoto each got a convertible—in the higher-priced series, as usual. Strong, and assembled with care using fine materials, they'd be remembered for their rust-resistance if nothing else. Sales reflected the dowdy, upright styling: The three makes combined managed just 6000 soft tops. Plymouth did the best with 3110, but Ford and Chevrolet sold 10 to 15 times as many, an indicator of the narrowing Plymouth appeal that would lead to a crisis at Chrysler by 1954.

The firm's most interesting '49 convertibles again carried Chrysler nameplates. The Windsor Six and New Yorker Eight were back, accompanied by a handsome New Yorker-based Town & Country. There was less wood than before, but the T&C remained a singular automobile. Counting 1000 of these, Chrysler sold nearly 5000 of its '49 convertibles.

A revolutionary 1949 development, the "hardtop convertible," gave Detroit soft tops new competition. The term came from GM, leading the way in styling innovations as usual—though Chrysler was nearly first with this one, having built seven prototype Town & Country hardtops in 1946, only to back away from production at the last minute.

No matter. The hardtop was an idea whose time had come: a convertible coupe with a roof that *didn't* convert.

Six convertibles from 1949. *Top row, from left:* Cadillac Series Sixty-Two, with a new 160-bhp V-8; Chrysler Town & Country, priced at a lofty $3970; one of the dramatically restyled Fords that trounced Chevy for the first time in years. *Bottom row, from left:* Frazer's four-door Manhattan, priced at $3295, found only about 70 buyers; $2952 Hudson Commodore 6; low-production Packard Super Eight.

Alternatively, it could be thought of as a traditional closed coupe *without* structural B-pillars. Either way, rolling down front and rear side windows made for a wide open space between top and beltline —and sportier looks than those of any pillared style. It also afforded much of the "airy" feel of convertibles combined with the superior rigidity, quietness, and convenience of a fixed steel roof.

To be sure, the hardtop was a compromise, but that was its very appeal: the best of both worlds. It wasn't long before the body style took off. By the mid-Fifties, the hardtop coupe, as some would call it, ranked second only to the mainstay four-door sedan as Detroit's most popular body style. Eventually it spawned four-door hardtop sedans and, in some model lines, even pillarless wagons.

It's thus instructive to record the hardtop's beginnings in 1949 with a trio of GM models: Buick Roadmaster Riviera, Cadillac Series 62 Coupe de Ville, and Oldsmobile 98 Holiday. All vied with corresponding convertibles as top of the line and were similarly trimmed, with leather upholstery and simulated chrome bows on headliners. Reflecting such finery, and perhaps the novelty of the idea, the Buick and Cadillac hardtops actually sold for a few dollars *more* than their ragtop sisters (the two Oldsmobiles cost the same). Production was accordingly limited—4343 Rivieras, 2150 Coupe de Villes, 3006 Holidays—though these were midyear introductions and thus in somewhat short supply. GM would correct both pricing and production in a big way for 1950.

Despite the hot breath of new competition, the convertible body style thrived in the decade ahead, as we'll see in our next chapter.

CHAPTER 3: 1950-1959
MORE AND LESS

GM was an industry leader throughout the Fifties, and had great success with convertibles. But the 1953 Olds Fiesta—priced at $5717—sold a mere 458 copies.

The Dodge Wayfarer gained roll-up windows in 1950 (*top*). A '50 Mercury convertible (*second from top*) could be had for $2412. Oldsmobile's 1950 88 (*third from top*) kicked off the division's aggressive convertible program for the decade. Pontiac's 1950 Chieftain Eight Deluxe (*bottom*) carried a 108-bhp straight eight.

The dominance of GM and Ford during the 1950s is precisely mirrored in convertible production. With one exception—1951, when Plymouth ranked fourth—Detroit's ragtop volume leaders were Ford, Chevrolet, Buick, Olds, and Pontiac.

And we're talking about really serious numbers of convertibles for the first time. Though output peaked in 1957 at over 300,000, the best year on a percentage basis was 1958, when soft tops grabbed an unusually high five-percent market share.

Then too, as the independent automakers failed or faltered, the Big Three moved to take their place, fielding more models and sub-models spanning ever-wider market sectors. Convertibles were naturally among them. Thus Ford Division, for example, which for years had gotten by with only one or two convertibles in the line, left the Fifties with three (and would have eight by 1966). If any period can be said to have been the convertible's "golden age," the 10 years beginning with 1957 was it.

Historically, the decade splits neatly in half: 1950-54, when most makers continued to update their initial postwar designs; and 1955-59, when higher horsepower and radical restyles were typically annual developments. Each period had one definite "check" year: 1952, when the Korean War curtailed civilian auto production; and 1958, when a recession cut deeply into car sales, giving imports their first firm toehold in the U.S. market and prompting the development of domestic compacts.

Ford remained the leader in convertible production for eight of these 10 years, 1950-57, while building some of the most radical topless models we'd ever see. Its approach through 1954 was straightforward: a single high-line soft top. All 1950-51 Fords were improved versions of the all-new make-or-break '49 design, with the convertible continuing in the upper-level Custom series. A chunky, well-built car on a 114-inch wheelbase, it was one the few Fords available only with V-8. Ford was onto something here. Few people wanted six-cylinder convertibles, and Ford's soft top usually outsold Chevy's two to one. Plymouth wisely paid heed and went the same route beginning with its '55 convertible.

Ford stole a big march on Chevy (which wouldn't be redesigned until '55) with its all-new '52, a fine piece of work by Frank Hershey, George Walker, and others. Though lower and smoother, boxy lines made it look otherwise despite an inch-longer wheelbase. The lineup expanded to three series. The convertible, newly designated the Sunliner, was in the top Crestline group, still with standard V-8. Base price was just over $2000. The Sunliner remained in this position through the extensive restyle of 1955-56, when it became part of the new top-line Fairlane series, named for Henry Ford's estate. By that point, Ford was offering a second convertible, a two-seater called Thunderbird.

Ordained by division general manager Lewis Crusoe and styled by Bill Boyer under Hershey's direction, the T-Bird was Ford's better mousetrap. Dearborn had looked hard at Chevrolet's 1953-54 Corvette and found it wanting. The Thunderbird would show what a two-seater should be. Ford made it a genuine convertible with roll-down windows and gave it a bolt-on hardtop for wintertime comfort (Corvette acquired these for '56). The 'Vette

body was fiberglass, the T-Bird's conventional steel. Early Corvettes had six-cylinder engines; the T-Bird bowed with a burly Mercury V-8, part of the new overhead-valve family that first appeared in Fords for '54. Also unlike the early Corvettes, manual transmissions were available.

Thunderbird's "boulevard sports car" concept worked: For debut '55, Ford's two-seater outsold Chevy's 24:1. But the rivalry ended almost as soon as it began. Corvette was transformed into a genuine sports car—and a convertible—for '56, while the Thunderbird became a four-seater—and a hardtop—after 1957. But the convertible remained, accounting for one of every seven T-Birds sold in 1959.

If the Thunderbird was romantic, Ford's 1957-59 retractable-hardtop Skyliner was exotic. Sharing Ford's all-new '57 platform, the biggest ever, the Skyliner had a huge steel roof that disappeared into a high, wide rear deck via a bevy of servo motors and miles of wiring. Even then, the top had to have a hinged front flap to fit, and left precious little trunk space when stowed. The "retrac" was expensive, too: over $400 more than the soft top Sunliner (both offered only in top-line Fairlane 500 trim). The price combined with mechanical problems to turn off customers, and production went from 20,766 for model-year '57 to 14,713 for '58, then to 12,915 for '59, after which the Skyliner was abandoned (at the bidding of division chief Robert S. McNamara) as a superfluous gimmick.

Clockwise from top left: Chevy's 1951 DeLuxe Styleline couldn't catch a comparable Ford, but still found 20,172 buyers; this prototype 1951 Kaiser ragtop was, regrettably, never produced; Mercury's '51 convertible sold for $2380; the Packard line was restyled for 1951 and offered a single convertible; Nash's 1951 Rambler convertible had an intriguing "roll back" top.

Mercury reverted from 1949-51's "small Lincoln" to its original status as a "big Ford" for 1952, then reached peak sales in 1955-57 with over 10,000 soft tops a year, making it seventh in convertibles after Ford and the five GM divisions. There was only one Mercury convertible through mid-decade, always in the most expensive series (Monterey for 1952-54, Montclair for '55). Beginning with the '56s, certain Mercury hardtops were called "Phaetons," though they were nothing of the sort.

That same year, Mercury began moving into Ford country with the low-price Medalist series and added a less costly convertible to the step-up Custom line, priced at $2712 (versus $2900 for the soft top Montclair). Mid-model-year '57 brought a third convertible, a roofless version of the glitzy Turnpike Cruiser.

Despite a raft of gimcracks including pushbutton Merc-O-Matic transmission—or perhaps because of them—only about 16,000 of the '57 Cruisers were built, of which 1265 were convertibles. The soft top vanished for 1958, when Turnpike Cruiser applied only to hardtops in a Montclair

subseries. The name was then consigned to the scrap heap as Mercury reverted to a three-series line with two convertibles, base Monterey and top-echelon Park Lane.

Lincoln's more dignified clients were habitually offered one convertible through the Fifties. The big, bulbous 1950-51 Cosmopolitans, with their curious "sad-eye" faces, saw very few copies (536 and 837, respectively). Cosmo was demoted to junior status for '52 and Capri came in to head the line, the ragtop remaining in the upper series. Convertible Capris saw somewhat higher volume than Cosmos but were no match for Cadillac; 2377 of the '53s was the best they'd ever do. Capri then moved down to make room for Premiere as the premium version of the wildly restyled, lower-longer-wider 1956 design; again, the convertible stayed in the senior series. Lincoln sold 2447 soft tops that year and 3676 of the '57s, the latter a record for the decade.

With dreams of rivaling GM as a multi-division producer, Ford formed a separate Continental Division to sell the $10,000 Mark II hardtop of 1956-57, then decided its impressive ultra-luxury car cost too much to build for what it brought in corporate prestige and showroom traffic. When Lincoln switched to a huge all-new unibody design for 1958, four Mark III derivatives were fielded as top-line models, though at much lower prices than the Mark II. Lincoln's convertible transferred to this line and sold at $6283; only 3048 were built. For 1959, Continental was folded back into a reconstituted Lincoln-Mercury Division and officially became a Lincoln again. That year's $7056 Mark IV convertible saw just 2195 copies.

Which brings us to Edsel, Ford Motor Company's ill-starred attempt at a second medium-price make. Though the very name has since become synonymous with "loser," Edsel wasn't nearly the failure people imagine it was. It cost Ford anywhere from $100 to $250 million—not exactly a drop in the bucket for even a big company, but no occasion for bankruptcy either—and it was not entirely unsaleable: 50,000 units wasn't bad in recession '58, Edsel's first model year.

Granted, Ford had planned for much more, invested heavily in plants and dealerships, and initially fielded no fewer than four Edsel series on three different wheelbases. There were two convertibles: the $3200 Pacer, a close cousin to that year's Ford, riding a 118-inch wheelbase; and the $4000 Citation, a Mercury relative on a 124-inch chassis. Despite gadgets galore and the Citation's jumbo 410-cid V-8 with 345 horsepower, Edsel convertible output was ridiculously low: 1876 Pacers, 930 Citations.

The 1959 Edsel line was drastically trimmed and all models made more like Fords. There was only one convertible, in the upper-series Corsair group, on a middling 120-inch wheelbase; 1343 were built. The Edsel died soon after the '60 models were announced. Again there was but one ragtop, in the remnant Ranger series. Production was a mere 76.

From top: Ford's completely redesigned 1952 Crestline Sunliner; Lincoln sold 1191 Capri convertibles for '52, each priced at $3665; like Ford, Mercury was restyled for '52, and offered this Monterey ragtop; Packard's 1952 output was limited by the Korean War, and included this 250 convertible; Pontiac offered six- and eight-cylinder versions of its convertible for '52—this red charmer is an eight.

FORD
OFFICIAL PACE CAR
500 MILE RACE MAY 30 1953

Top row, from left: Buick scored with this '53 Super; Cadillac's '53 Eldorado ragtop sold 532 units at $7750 apiece. *Second row, from left:* The sedate but appealing '53 DeSoto Firedome; 1953 Dodge Coronet, with the 140-bhp "Red Ram" V-8. *Above:* 1953 Ford Crestline replica of that year's Indy 500 pace car. *Far left:* The substantial-looking '53 Plymouth Cranbrook convertible found 6301 buyers at $2220. *Left:* Pontiac added tiny tailfins for '53, as on this Chieftain.

Though Ford Division was the dominant make in Fifties convertible sales, General Motors was the decade's big gun in corporate convertible volume. Four of its brands—Chevrolet and the B-O-P nameplates—usually ran 2-5, and even Cadillac was no slouch, averaging about 10,000 topless cars a year.

Cadillac built some of GM's most interesting Fifties convertibles, certainly the most expensive. Through 1952, the division continued with a single Series 62 model that tallied about 6500 units a year. For 1953, Cadillac added the Motorama-inspired Eldorado, essentially a 62 with custom interior, cut-down "Panoramic" wrapped windshield, distinctive notched beltline, and a metal instead of canvas cover for the stowed top. The Eldo wasn't intended to make a profit—and at $7750 and only 532 units, the '53 didn't. Instead, its role was to bring in customers for the ordinary models, which it did.

But when Cadillac restyled for '54, the game plan changed. Cut $2000 in price, the Eldorado went all out for

Buick's 1954 Super (*top left*) enticed buyers with new slab-sided styling and a $2964 price tag. Buick's '54 Skylark (*top right*) was even snappier—and pricier, too: $4483. Cadillac's Eldorado (*above*) became longer, lower, and wider for '54.

sales: 2150 found buyers that year, thus establishing the model as a limited-production money-spinner. By 1955, Eldorados wore their own special "shark-fin" rear fenderlines; a year later came an Eldorado Seville hardtop to match the convertible, now called Biarritz.

Eldorados were technically part of the Series 62 until 1959, when they were broken out as a separate group. Combined, the Eldo and Series 62 put Cadillac convertible volume into five figures for the first time in 1955, a level that was usually maintained in subsequent years. The Eldo was heroically overdecorated next to the 62, glistening with chrome and $2000 more expensive. But though never intended for high volume, it did account for up to 20 percent of Cadillac's convertible production.

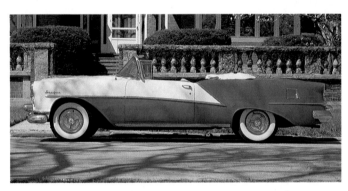

Top row, from left: Dodge produced 710 Indy pace-car replica convertibles for 1954; the '54 Hudson Hornet was a handsome variant of the "Step-down" design. *Middle row, from left:* Nash's cute Metropolitan debuted for '54; Olds's 1954 Starfire went for $3249. *Bottom row, from left:* Only 863 "standard" Packard ragtops found homes in 1954; 400 of the gorgeous '54 Packard Caribbeans were sold.

In convertibles as most other matters, Cadillac outdid Lincoln as well as Packard, the latter at one time a rival to both makes but fated to a sad death in 1957-58, following a poorly executed partnership deal with Studebaker. Until the 1952 arrival of James Nance as company president, Packard had built convertibles almost as afterthoughts: a handful of dumpy Supers and Customs in 1950, then a series of short-wheelbase 250s on the junior (Clipper) body for 1951-53. The latter were nice, well built, and reliable—and utterly boring. At $3400-$3500, they were more competitive with Buick and Chrysler than Cadillac.

Setting out to recapture past glories, Nance asked stylist Dick Teague to create a limited-edition soft top for 1953. The result was the Caribbean, with handsome, clean-limbed open-wheel styling and a 180-bhp straight eight. At $5210, it was $2500 cheaper than the Eldo and thus handily outsold it. But Packard hit the skids in 1954, planning to bring out a new line but settling for a facelift. Only 400 of the '54 Caribbeans and 863 conventional convert-

ibles were sold, all still with the junior body on its relatively short chassis.

But Nance got his big restyle for '55, including a lavish new Caribbean on the long wheelbase at last. It was Packard's only soft top that year, priced at $6000.

Packard had a fair year in 1955 but fell apart in 1956. Customers deserted what they perceived was a failing brand and dealers bailed out in favor of Big Three franchises while the factory nursed quality control and production problems. The '56 Caribbean was a fabulous car, and its reversible seat cushion covers (leather on one side, cloth the other) were a novel touch, but just 276 were built. Even then, there were leftovers.

Returning to General Motors, we find a vast range of convertibles in the popular Buick, Olds, and Pontiac lines spanning the decade's wide medium-price sector.

Buick, usually the industry's leading convertible maker in the Forties, fell behind in the Fifties as Ford and Chevy volume soared. But Buick continued to place great emphasis on soft tops. It began the decade with three, reviving a Super to complement Special and Roadmaster models, then wowed the public in 1953 with the handsome $5000 Skylark, a sort of Buick Eldorado.

The Skylark was the most successful of 1953's three limited-edition GM convertibles, seeing 1690 units compared to only 532 Cadillac Eldorados and 458 Olds Fiestas. The '54 Skylark was more conventional and rather gaudy, complete with big, tack-on chrome tailfins. After only 836 of these, the Skylark was retired.

No matter. Buick was destined for bigger things, notably a production surge that would take it ahead of Plymouth into third place behind Chevrolet and Ford. This was achieved in calendar-year '54 and model-year 1955. Reflecting its exuberance, Buick offered no fewer than five 1954 convertibles: the aforementioned Skylark, the usual Special/Super/Roadmaster trio, and one in the newly revived Century series. Prices ranged from the $2563 for the Special to $3521 for the Roadmaster. Arguably most desirable was the hot-rod $2963 Century, with the big 200-horsepower 322-cubic-inch Roadmaster V-8 in the lighter, short-wheelbase Special body. A well-tuned Century ragtop could do 0-60 mph in 10 seconds and 110 mph flat out. No wonder Buick sold about 5000 a year in 1955-57 at prices in the $3000-$3600 range.

A revised '58 Buick lineup saw the Super series trimmed and a new Limited version of the Roadmaster, priced $500 higher. Buick retained four convertibles, a Limited model replacing the previous Super, but these garish cruisers were the wrong cars for a recession year. The '59 Buicks were locked up before that became apparent, but were much better cars nevertheless: smooth if flamboyant, and well engineered. They were also renamed, with convertibles in the LeSabre, Invicta, and Electra 225 series at base prices of $3200-$4200.

Oldsmobile followed a more modest convertible program, fielding a 98 and Super 88 (plain 88 for '50) through 1956 (plus 973 tail-end 76 convertibles in 1950). The aforementioned '53 Fiesta, a semi-show car in the 98 line, was priced too high to sell ($5717) and vanished after just one year.

After zooming to fourth in the industry by 1955, Olds confidently launched a restyled line of 1957 "Golden Rockets" that included 88, Super 88, and 98 convertibles. All continued through 1959 and notched combined output of up to 22,000 a year.

Pontiac, too, was far more flush by mid-decade, moving from its traditional sixth to the number-five slot. Through 1953 it cataloged two soft tops: a Six and Eight on identical wheelbases. The Six finished up in '54 and a new straight-eight Star Chief series arrived with that year's only Pontiac convertible. Things would stay this way until 1958, when a second ragtop, in the baseline Chieftain series, was added.

These were nothing like the convertible-only Bonneville, introduced as a midyear '57 model and equipped

with a 347-cid V-8 version that packed 300 bhp via fuel injection, hydraulic lifters, and racing cam. It made for the fastest Pontiac yet—faster still with optional Tri-Power (three two-barrel carbs), able to scorch through the quarter-mile in 16.8 seconds. A $6000 price made for only 630 sales in the first year, but a newly styled and more affordable '58 ($3586) sold 3096. For 1959, still sharing bodyshells with Chevrolet but with its own distinctive styling, Pontiac made Bonneville its new top-line series, adding a wagon and hardtop sedan to the previous convertible and hardtop coupe. More than 11,000 of the droptops were sold.

Against V-8 Fords, Chevrolet had always had an uphill battle for convertible sales. As noted, its 1950-54 line of good-looking but low-powered six-cylinder cars never approached Ford's volume. But things began to change with the '55s, which were the best Chevys yet and, as many agree, some of the best American cars ever built. They also ushered in Chevy's first modern V-8, the excellent 265 small-block, shepherded into production by chief engineer Ed Cole.

Suddenly, "Chevrolet" meant "performance," and a Bel Air convertible was the hottest low-price car around. No surprise, as the '55 Ford was a heavily facelifted '54, while

Opposite page, from top: The 331-cid V-8 in the 1955 Cadillac Series 62 convertible was good for 250 bhp; the all-new '55 Chevy shocked Chevy's competitors and thrilled buyers with the likes of this convertible Bel Air; Chrysler also received a smart restyle for '55—this aggressive-looking convertible is a Fireflyte with a 200-bhp V-8. *This page, clockwise from top left:* This 1955 Dodge Royal Lancer not only shows off a redesign, but an unusual two-tone paint combination; 1955 brought the first Ford Thunderbird, an enduring classic; Oldsmobile's '55 Super 88 found 9007 buyers; an impressively restyled Caribbean was Packard's only convertible for 1955, but found just 500 buyers; Pontiac's top-line '55 Star Chief had a new, 180-bhp V-8; Plymouth's '55 Belvedere had V-8s good for up to 177 bhp; the premier Mercury offering for '55 was the 198-bhp V-8 Montclair.

the '55 Chevy was all-new and beautifully styled, built with care, and available in a raft of colors (including handsome two-tones). It only got better through the deft Cadillac-like restyles of 1956 and '57, and Impala sales continued to be robust for 1958 and '59.

Meantime, the Chevy Corvette had gone from sales chump to sports-car champ, partly by adopting convertible features. They first appeared on the '56s, along with curvy new styling that completely did away with the former "bathtub" look. The '57s were outwardly unchanged but went faster, thanks to that year's enlarged, 283-cid small-block and optional fuel injection that produced 283 horsepower. Handling improved too. A bulkier, weightier body with four headlamps and more chrome made the '58 aesthetically less pleasing, but performance wasn't affected and volume went up. The '59s were treated to a minor cleanup and tallied 9670 units, a long way from the 3467 Corvettes built for '56. Chevy's sports car was here to stay.

Plymouth trailed badly in convertible production, not only behind the Big Two but the other GM makes and Mercury, as well. Plymouth's conservative image was a liability *vis à vis* convertible appeal, so the marque rode a roller coaster in the Fifties. After Detroit's dullest '49 restyle, its 1950-52 models were little different and their 1953-54 revisions weren't much better. The '55 was something else, though: shapely, colorful, and eye-catching, the work of Maury Baldwin and Virgil Exner. Plymouth was all-new again just two years later—the style leader of the Low-Price Three—and its V-8s were at least a match for the competition's. But soft top sales didn't budge, perhaps because the ragtop received no marketing emphasis. Even

Plymouth's hottest, the 1956-58 Fury, came only as a hardtop coupe.

Through 1958, Plymouth offered only one convertible, in the top-line series as usual: Special Deluxe (1950), Cranbrook (1951-53), Belvedere (1954-58). With such low volume, it made sense to standardize the V-8 for '55. The '57s were dramatic-looking and very impressive, the convertible wearing a special compound-curve windshield wrapped up at the top as well as around to the sides.

A second Plymouth convertible arrived for 1959 as a companion for that year's new Sport Fury hardtop, with up to 305 horsepower from a ram-induction 361-cid "Golden Commando" V-8. Big and flashy, the Sport Fury was what convertible buyers wanted and claimed over half of Plymouth's ragtop output that year, which itself was the highest since 1950.

Dodge was equally dull in the early Fifties but more interesting than Plymouth, thanks to several unique models. One bowed with the new low-price Wayfarer series of 1949: an open three-seater with side curtains, which was thus technically a roadster. For 1950 it acquired roll-up windows to become a convertible, and looked more "important." Sales were never significant: 2903 of the '50s, 1002 of the '51s.

The standard Dodge convertible of these years was always in the premium Coronet series, which received the new "Red Ram" 241 V-8 for 1953. The name changed to Royal for '54, when 2000 were built. Included were 701 Royal 500s, hot machines in the image of that year's Indi-

Top row, from left: Distinctive fins characterized the 1956 Cadillac Eldorado Biarritz; Chevy continued its winning ways in '56 with the Bel Air ragtop. *Second row, from left:* The 1956 El Morocco was a minuscule-production Chevy-based oddity that brought Caddy-like styling touches to the smaller platform, courtesy of Detroit entrepreneur Ruben Allender; Lincoln's Premier, emphatically restyled for '56, was priced at $4747. *Third row, from left:* The 1956 Mercury Custom convertible came in at $2712; Plymouth's '56 Belvedere went out the door for $2478. *Left:* The top-line Star Chief was Pontiac's only convertible for 1956.

Top row, from left: Buick's Roadmaster became gaudier for 1957; the '57 Cadillac Eldorado, priced at $7286, wasn't exactly subdued, either; Chrysler's legendary 300C had Virgil Exner's new "Forward Look" styling, and available horsepower up to a thumping 390. *Above:* More of Chrysler Corporation's forward-looking styling, seen here on a 1957 DeSoto Adventurer.

anapolis pace car, supplied with chrome wire wheels, continental spare tire, special badges, and a 150-bhp Red Ram. Dealers could even specify a four-barrel Offenhauser manifold that made this somewhat dumpy droptop a genuine scorcher.

With a snazzy 1955 facelift, Dodge, like Plymouth, became a serious competitor again. From 1956 through 1959 there were always two convertibles, Coronet and Custom Royal—three if we count 1957's new D-500 option, available on any model in the line. This brought a firm suspension, a 245-bhp hemi V-8, and 0-60-mph times of around nine seconds. The bold and rapid D-500 continued for 1958-59, though a wedgehead engine replaced the hemi. Offered with fuel injection for 1958, the 361-cid wedge produced 333 bhp, a new Dodge high.

DeSoto persisted with one upper-echelon convertible through 1954, then expanded in a big way: a Fireflite and Firedome for '55, a special Fireflite Pacesetter for mid-'56 (100 replicas of that year's Indy pacer), a new Adventurer model for '57, and four different soft tops—Firesweep, Firedome, Fireflite, and Adventurer—for 1958-59. Then . . .

nothing, as DeSoto's final offering was a truncated line of sedans and hardtops for 1960-61.

The wildest DeSotos were the pre-1960 Adventurers, limited-production jobs with arresting color combinations, acres of anodized aluminum trim, and the hairiest engines (in '57, for instance, a 345-cid hemi with one bhp per cubic inch). Convertible production was very limited: 300 of the '57s, 82 for '58, and just 97 of the '59s—now collector's items all. They could fly, too: Fast-shifting Torque-Flite automatic took most Adventurers from 0 to 60 mph in around seven seconds and on to 125 mph or more. Torsion-bar front suspension gave these big bruisers surprisingly good handling.

Lesser DeSoto ragtops were hardly more numerous. In fact, the highest production for any V-8 DeSoto convertible came with the 1956 Fireflite: just 1385. Others are counted in the hundreds.

Chrysler Corporation is a leading convertible-maker today. But as the foregoing makes clear, its soft top business was peripheral in the Fifties. This was true even for the high-priced Chrysler and Imperial, which had always

done well with ragtops. Chrysler consistently offered two models, Windsor and New Yorker, through 1956, plus an Imperial version for '51. Annual volume, though, was measured in four small figures. It remained so for 1957, when the soft top Windsor was replaced by the first convertible 300, a muscle car of impeccable breeding.

The '57 Chryslers were among Virgil Exner's best designs, gracefully finned and beautifully clean—though nobody knew then how quickly they could rust. Hemi V-8s and torsion-bar front suspension made them among the most roadable cars in America. The 300C convertible, with up to 390 bhp, high-grade interior, and unique frontal styling, listed at $5359 (close to $6000 delivered); just 484 were built. The following year's 300D notched only 191 convertible sales, and 1959's wedgehead 300E scored just 140. The New Yorker, slightly less lavish but more affordable ($4600-$4900), fared little better: for 1957-59 respectively, 1049, 666, and 286.

Imperial became a separate make for 1955 but wasn't offered as a convertible until 1957. That happened to be Imperial's best year ever, the only one in which it would

Top row, from left: Unique to Dodge's '57 models were "swept wing" tailfins, as on this Coronet; Ford's restyled '57s included the Fairlane 500; that same model year brought the last of the two-seat Thunderbirds. *Second row, from left:* Heavy, overdone styling marked the '57 Mercury Turnpike Cruiser, seen here in Indy pace-car replica guise; the reskinned '57 Oldsmobile had a 371-cid 277-bhp V-8 as standard. *Bottom row:* 1957 Pontiac Star Chief with a 290-bhp V-8; Bonneville joined the Poncho lineup for '57.

outsell Lincoln. Helping were 1167 Crown convertibles at $5568 apiece. From then on, the soft top languished at 500-700 units a year as one ornate facelift succeeded another.

The Fifties were disastrous for all the independents. Packard's fate has already been mentioned. Partner Studebaker almost died with it, but was rescued at the eleventh hour (in 1958) by Curtiss-Wright, mainly as a tax loss.

Studebaker had cut out convertibles well before its mid-decade crisis. Its only Fifties soft tops were thus the little Raymond Loewy Champions and somewhat larger Commanders of 1950-52. The Commander received a fine new

Top row, from left: $5125 1958 Buick Limited; $7500 '58 Cadillac Eldorado Biarritz. *Second row, from left:* $3219 1958 DeSoto Firesweep; $3298 '58 Dodge Royal Lancer. *Third row, from left:* $3801 1958 Edsel Citation; $6283 '58 Lincoln Continental Mark III. *Above:* $3529 1958 Oldsmobile Super 88. *Right:* $3586 1958 Pontiac Bonneville.

V-8 for 1951, which gave its convertible real performance. What it needed was real styling. Studey was still plying its basic 1947 design, made bizarre with the "bullet-nose" facelift of 1950-51, more acceptable with the "clam-digger" front of 1952 (the firm's centennial year). Relative to its size, Studebaker sold a fair number of convertibles.

Nash built no large convertibles after 1948, but did produce a popular little one, the six-cylinder Rambler, which arrived in 1950 and was also offered as a two-door station wagon. Though its window frames were fixed and only the top dropped, the roofless Rambler won people over, perhaps because, at $1808, it was 1950's least expensive convertible. A total of 9330 were built for the model year. The convertible remained in production through 1954; its price was up to only $1980 by then.

Arriving in 1954 to succeed Nash's small convertible was an even smaller one: the three-passenger Metropolitan, which also came as a coupe. Built in England with an Austin engine but resolutely Nash in appearance, the petite 85-inch-wheelbase Met enjoyed its greatest popularity in 1959, when more than 22,000 were sold, about a third of them soft tops.

A few Metropolitans were also badged as Hudsons following the 1954 merger of Hudson and Nash. It's unclear when the last of these were sold, but the car simply became "Metropolitan" once Nash and Hudson expired in '57. Technically then, this was Hudson's last convertible. The big ones had ended in 1954. The last recorded production for Hudson soft tops is 1952, when it listed 636.

All this is strange in a way, because Hudson seemed a strong proponent of convertibles. For 1950 it had no fewer than five: Pacemaker and Pacemaker Deluxe on a new 119-inch wheelbase; Super Six and Commodore Six/Eight on the familiar 124. The line was rearranged for 1951 and the potent Hornet arrived; it, too, was offered as a convertible, called "Brougham" (as were all droptop Hudsons in this period).

The last of Kaiser-Frazer's unique convertible sedans were offered as 1951 Frazer Manhattans. These were basically leftover 1950 Kaisers and Frazers "restyled" with new front and rear ends. Surveys of survivors suggest original production of between 128 and 131. Why so few? A hefty $3075 price and a face only their mother could love. It was a salvage operation anyway, intended to rid K-F of remaining old-style bodies. Ironically, dealers could have sold 50,000 of the peculiar '51 Frazers, but only 10,000 were built in all.

As for Kaiser, its second-generation design for 1951 was all-new and beautiful, again the work of the artistic Dutch Darrin. A prototype convertible was built, but the company would never have the funds to get one into production. Ditto hardtops, station wagons, and V-8s. These deficits, plus Henry Kaiser's intransigence and the money-sapping Henry J compact, culminated in 1955 with the departure of Kaiser-Willys from the U.S. car market.

Despite the unhappy fates of so many independent automakers during the Fifties, the decade shines as a high point in convertible development and marketing. Often beautiful, sometimes outlandish, the ragtops of the Fifties epitomize a remarkable period of American vigor and self-confidence; little wonder that these cars are so coveted today.

Buick's top-line Electra 225 convertible (*top*) offered dramatic styling and a 325-bhp V-8 for $4192. The '59 Dynamic 88 (*second from top*) was the best-selling Olds ragtop for the model year. Mile-high tailfins rose from the '59 Plymouth Sport Fury (*third from top*). Pontiac's '59 Catalina (*bottom*) had a "Tri-Power" V-8.

Chapter 4: 1960-1969
Chutes and Ladders

The horsepower wars escalated in the Sixties; convertibles like this hot 1965 Chevy Impala SS went along for the ride.

For Detroit, the Sixties was the greatest decade yet. Nineteen sixty-five saw a new yearly production record that would not be surpassed until 1974; 1966 and 1969 were almost as good, and annual volume was never under seven million cars after 1962.

The Sixties were also the best years for American convertibles. Over half a millon were built in '65, a record that will probably never be equaled, let alone topped. Their heyday was 1962-66, when ragtops enjoyed a six-percent market share, up from only 4.5 percent in 1960.

Yet in the end, the Sixties was a giant game of Chutes and Ladders: By 1969, the convertible's market penetration had been cut by half. A few years later, soft top models would account for less than one percent of all Detroit cars.

The Sixties convertible leaders were remarkably constant. With one exception, the top five producers were always the same: Chevrolet, Ford, Pontiac, Buick; and Oldsmobile, which finished in that order in five of the 10 model years. The exception was 1961, when Cadillac built a few more convertibles than Olds. In 1965-66, largely on the strength of its popular new Mustang, Ford managed to build more soft tops than Chevy. Once the "ponycar" craze subsided, though, Chevrolet was again the convertible leader, and in 1968-69, Pontiac ran second, ahead of Ford.

Top row, from left: The 1960 Buick Electra 225 had 325 bhp and went for $4192; the 1960 Buick LeSabre ran with 250 bhp and was priced at $3145. *Middle row, from left:* Cadillac's tailfins diminished slightly for 1960, as on this $7401 Eldorado Biarritz; Chevy's '60 Impala rivaled the Caddy for glitz. *Bottom row, from left:* The Super 88 was the fastest of three Olds ragtops offered for 1960; the '60 Pontiac Bonneville convertible found 17,172 buyers; unibody construction distinguished the '60 Plymouth Fury.

Independents were hardly in the convertible business during the Sixties, mainly because there were hardly any independents left. Let's begin with their story.

Studebaker-Packard (renamed Studebaker Corporation in 1962) returned to convertibles for 1960 with a compact Lark offering, its first soft top in eight years. At 8571 units, model-year production was rather good, considering the South Bend automaker hadn't built more than that many convertibles a year since 1950. But the pace wouldn't last.

Styled by Duncan McRae, the pert and practical Lark was a clever shortened and reskinned update of Studebaker's old 1953-58 sedan/wagon platform (several years of huge deficits precluded an all-new design). It arrived for 1959, when people were turning away from Detroit dinosaurs and toward imports, notably the seemingly preposterous Volkswagen. Big Three compacts were then a year off, so Studebaker shared the domestic small-car market only with Rambler, which was doing even better.

People who wouldn't have been caught dead in a Studebaker showroom a year earlier scrambled to buy Larks in '59. Calendar-year production rose from 45,000 in 1958 to over 126,000, and Studebaker made an unaccustomed profit.

The Lark was a good product, available with Studebaker's old L-head six or its somewhat younger and still spunky 259 V-8. From the first, Studebaker wisely offered several body styles: two-door wagon, hardtop coupe, and two- and four-door sedans. The new-for-'60 convertible came only in upmarket Regal trim at starting prices of $2600-$2700. The '61 version was little changed apart from slightly squarer contours.

Unfortunately, neither the convertible nor the Lark line as a whole could maintain their strong initial sales. Between formidable rivalry from the Falcon/Corvair/Valiant trio and certain problems of its own, Studebaker could only watch its sales plunge.

For 1962, Studebaker added a bucket-seat V-8 convertible called Daytona, then put the label on all its '63 ragtops. But by then, the Big Three compacts all had convertibles too, and each undercut the Daytona's price. Studey convertible volume thus hovered around 2000 units for 1961-62, dropped to 1000 for '63, then to only 703 of the '64s, all V-8 Daytonas. Studebaker convertibles, and a good many other models, were dropped for 1965-66, when the firm departed South Bend and consolidated operations at its Canadian plant in Hamilton, Ontario. After that, Studebaker abandoned cars altogether.

Rambler enjoyed much higher volume and a much better public image than Studebaker, George Romney's American Motors surprising just about everybody—including Romney—in the late Fifties. By 1960, Rambler was fourth in overall volume at well over 400,000 cars. In 1961 it displaced Plymouth as number three, then built a record 428,346 cars in 1963 (though that was good for only eighth in the industry that year).

Rambler's sole convertible for 1961-63 was a 100-inch-wheelbase American model, attractively tagged at around $2400 base. The original 1958 American was a resurrected, slightly restyled 1953-55 Nash Rambler, a recession-market emergency measure. The '61 was simply a reskinned version, styled by craggy AMC chief designer Edmund Anderson, and intended to keep the old design going a few more years. A new convertible and hardtop coupe were part of the plan. But aesthetically, it didn't work; the cars looked very boxy and truncated, prompting one English designer hired by AMC to compare them to ordnance vehicles.

Nevertheless, the American convertible turned a profit, recording 13,497 sales for '62 (the only year for which we could find sales figures). Far more efficient than expiring Studebaker, AMC was able to build this convertible to a price competitive with those of Valiant, Falcon, and Corvair models. That was the key to its success, along with the parent company's hearty reputation at the time.

Completely restyled by Dick Teague on a six-inch longer wheelbase, the '64 added good styling to the American's list of attributes. Though bucket-seat hardtops had been available for a couple of years, the convertible continued in the mid-range bench-seat 440 series, priced at $2346.

Buick sliced off its tailfins for 1961, as on this LeSabre (*top*)—and saw sales decline. Cadillac offered two convertibles for 1961: the $5455 Series 62 (*second from top*) and the $6477 Eldorado Biarritz. Rakish styling continued on the '61 Chevy Impala (*third from top*). Chrysler's 1961 New Yorker (*above*) sold 576 copies.

Top: Odd, pod-like fender and taillight treatment distinguished the 1961 Dodge Polara from other convertibles. *Middle row, from left:* Ford built 44,614 befinned Sunliners for 1961; sister make Mercury's '61 Monterey sported similar tailfins; the fins were modified into free-standing

taillamps on the '62 Mercs. *Bottom row, from left:* The virtues—and beauty—of simplicity were obvious in the lines of the '61 Lincoln Continental, the first American convertible sedan in a decade; the 1961 Olds Starfire could be purchased for $4647.

With the convertible suddenly a serious salesmaker for the first time in anyone's memory, AMC decided to add Classic and Ambassador soft tops for '65. Both lines were cleanly restyled that year, and the latter was stretched to 116 inches between wheel centers, 200 inches overall (a size that would have been anathema to Romney, who had been succeeded by Roy Abernethy in 1962). AMC called its '65s the "Sensible Spectaculars," but convertible sales weren't rousing: 12,334 for the three models combined.

Ambassador was officially a Rambler series through 1965, then registered as a separate AMC "make." Otherwise, the company's '66 convertibles were the same: one American, one Classic, one Ambassador. Classic became a Rebel for '67, and along with Ambassador acquired smooth new "Coke-bottle" styling, one of Teague's best (and still underappreciated) efforts. Responding to the era's sporty-car craze, the American convertible became a bucket-seat Rogue ($2600 base) that year and the former Classic 770 was similarly transformed into a Rebel SST ($2800). The '67 droptop Ambassador appeared in the lush, top-line DPL series ($3143).

Only the Rebel remained for 1968 (when that name achieved make status too), though a base-series 550 convertible arrived ($2736), perhaps to make up for the loss of the American. Respective production was just 377 and 823 units. These would be AMC's last convertibles until the soft top Renault Alliance of 17 years later.

Turning to the Big Three, Chrysler (the make) never seemed able to sustain its previous soft top success in the Sixties. Indeed, the production record suggests that those who've glommed on to certain offerings had better keep them; there probably aren't that many left. Production of the 1960 through '65 300 letter-series convertibles never topped 625 per year, a peak reached in 1964; the '62 300H droptop is particularly rare, as only 123 were made. Even some of the more "mundane" Chrysler convertibles were built in very limited numbers. Any 1960 or '61 New Yorker, for instance, would have fewer than 575 sister ships. All the hot-performing letter-series 300s were memorable, none more than the convertibles, available each year from 1957 through '65 except 1963. Regrettably, the series became rather tame toward the end, much closer to ordinary Chryslers in appearance, features, and performance. Then again, 1962's mighty 300H could be had with 405 horsepower, enough to blow away most any rival. And on its firm, race-bred suspension it could embarrass many a foreign sports car.

Cast in the letter-series image was a standard 300 series that replaced the mid-range Windsor for 1962. Engines were smaller and bucket seats cost extra, but prices were much lower and styling a dead ringer for that of the letter cars. These 300s were more successful, though not a lot. The most numerous of the convertibles were the '63s, which sold about 3400 units, including 1861 specially trimmed "Pace Setter" models.

A "Sportsgrain" option for the 1968 300s, a swathe of pseudo-wood trim along the bodyside, was installed on 175 convertibles. And for non-letter, low-line ragtop fun, Chrysler offered a Windsor for 1960, and a Newport for the rest of the decade. (When these non-letter cars arrived, the long-running New Yorker convertible was dropped. It had never sold well.)

The pinnacle of GM's convertible lineup for 1962 was the $6477 Cadillac Eldorado Biarritz (*top*). The lower limit was represented by the handsome Chevy II Nova 400 (*second from top*) at $2475. Ford's '62 Galaxie 500/XL Sunliner (*third from top*) had a 170-bhp 292-cid V-8. Plymouth's '62 Sport Fury (*above*) sold for $3082.

Of course, Chrysler-Plymouth dealers had the even bigger Imperial convertibles to sell in these years, but they didn't sell many. The peak was 1964, with production of 922 units. These flashy land yachts invariably appeared in the Crown series, a step up from the base Custom through 1963, the standard Imperial series thereafter. Unlike other Chrysler products, Imperial retained a separate body and chassis until 1967, when production economics dictated a switch to unit construction. With that, Imperial increasingly became less distinctive and more a glorified Chrysler. Convertibles were the most expensive Imps short of the plush LeBaron hardtops and rarified Crown Imperial limos, selling well into the $6000-$7000 range—which at least partly accounts for their low volume.

A downsizing of Dodge and Plymouth models for the 1962 model year killed sales, which did not recover until 1963's emphasis on a longer wheelbase and improved V-8 power (including the competition-proven 426 hemi).

Big Dodge convertibles for 1960-61 comprised Polara and Dart Phoenix models; 1962's were the mid-size Dart 440 and bucket-seat Polara 500, plus a big Custom 880. The Dart name replaced Lancer on Dodge's 1963 compact, which offered convertibles in mid-range 270 and bucket-seat GT trim. Priced under $3000, they were quite popular. Pushing hard at a sporty image, Dodge had no fewer than seven convertibles by 1965, its best year: the two Darts; Polara and Custom 880 models on a new 119-inch-wheelbase platform; and three in the mid-size Coronet line, a renamed, restyled '62 evolution. This broad allotment continued through the rest of the decade (and some confusing name changes).

Buick's 1963 LeSabre ragtop (*top left*) was a solid seller at 9975 units. Chevy's V-8 powered '63 Impala SS convertible (*top right*) staked out aggressive styling territory. Fin shrinkage continued at Cadillac for 1963, as on this Eldorado Biarritz (*above*).

One of Dodge's nicest Sixties ragtops was the intermediate Coronet R/T ("Road/Track") of 1967, an even livelier version of the previous year's good-looking, restyled Coronet 500. Standard equipment included bucket-seat interior, a 375-horsepower 440 V-8, heavy-duty "handling" suspension, wide tires, and oversize brakes. The hemi was technically available, having been reinstated as a production option for '66, but relatively few R/Ts were so equipped.

The Plymouth convertible story mirrors Dodge's. While Dodge production totals are largely unavailable, it seems that Plymouth built more open cars. Plymouth's first-generation Valiant (1960-62) wasn't offered as a convertible, but when the popular compact was redesigned for 1963 (along with Dodge's), it received two, a standard V200 and a bucket-seat Signet.

Plymouth's finest convertibles were reserved for the Fury line: full-size for 1960-61, mid-size for 1962-64, "standard" again from 1965. Beginning with 1962, a second ragtop was offered under the revived Sport Fury name, a swashbuckling bucket-seat performer with standard V-8. Two more convertibles arrived with the intermediate Belvedere/Satellite group of 1965, riding the 116-inch wheelbase deserted by Fury. Sharing their basic engineering with the Dodge Coronet, they were good-looking cars with squarish lines, clean sides, and lots of glass. The

Satellite two-door convertible and hardtop topped the Belvedere line and, like Coronet, could be ordered with a 426 wedgehead V-8 developing 365 bhp and 470 pounds/feet torque.

The memorable Belvedere GTX arrived for 1967 as a convertible and hardtop coupe with standard 440 V-8 (hemi optional), silver-and-black grille and rear-deck appliqué, simulated hood air intakes, sport striping, dual exhausts, and buckets-and-console cabin. GTXs weren't cheap—$3500 base, around $4300 with typical options—but they were elegant muscle cars, among the best of that breed.

And for budget muscle in 1968, there was the new Road Runner, basically a no-frills GTX with a standard 383 V-8, firm suspension, and heavy-duty manual transmission. By 1969, the RR convertible was available, priced at $3313; 2128 copies were sold, compared to more than 82,000 coupes and hardtops.

Plymouth's one other convertible in this decade arrived with the second-generation Barracuda of 1967-69, a more aggressive-looking car than the Valiant-based first generation. Although the 383 V-8 was newly available, the lighter, higher-revving 273 small-block was a better choice for street work.

Convertibles were the least salesworthy of the second-generation Barracudas, generating only 4228 orders for '67, 2840 for '68, and 1442 for '69. But that's the kind of volume that excites collectors, and the package itself was a good one.

At Ford, the 1960 model year brought the Continental Mark V, a continuation of the 1958-59 Mark III/IV, Lin-

Chrysler paced the 1963 Indianapolis 500, and celebrated the event with replica Chrysler 300 convertibles (*top left*). Rocket-like 1963 Ford Thunderbird (*top right*), with optional tonneau cover. The $4742 Olds Starfire convertible (*above left*) was the most expensive Olds for 1963. Less pricey open-air motoring was offered by the $2564 '63 Pontiac Tempest (*above right*).

coln-Mercury's attempt at a less costly, more saleable ultra-luxury car that would actually make money. As ever, the convertible was the most expensive model apart from the limousine, base-priced at around $7000. It tallied only 2044 units.

But even as the first of these monsters was being introduced for 1958, the decision had been made to design an all-new Lincoln. When this appeared for 1961, the giant square-rigged Marks (and related standard Lincolns) were dropped. (The Mark III tag would return, however, gracing a much smaller new 1968 personal-luxury hardtop.)

The '61 Lincoln Continental arrived in two four-door body styles: hardtop and convertible. The crisp, chiseled styling was immediately apparent; dead-on, the windows sloped inward toward the roof—the greatest "tumblehome" yet seen on an American car and one of the first uses of curved side glass in regular production.

Unlike Kaiser-Frazer's convertible sedans, the Lincoln's side glass and window frames completely disappeared for a pure, uncluttered look. Likewise its convertible top, which stowed Ford Skyliner-style beneath a hinged rear deck via 11 relays connecting various mechanical and hydraulic linkages. Workmanship was first-rate. Customers also benefited from the industry's most thorough pre-

delivery testing and a then-unprecedented two-year/ 24,000-mile warranty.

As ever, though, the convertible was more indulgence than salesmaker, never amounting to more than about 10 percent of Continental production. It thus came to an end after '67 and the lowest convertible volume for the 1964-67 design generation: only 2276 units.

Mercury, Lincoln's "other half," played a supporting role in the division's Sixties convertible business. Mercury soft top production (all two-doors) peaked with the '63s: over 18,000, a record that still stands. But dealers never seemed to push convertibles very hard, nor were the cars particularly innovative.

Mercury's early-Sixties big convertibles were peripheral low-volume models: a Monterey and Park Lane for 1960 (about 7500 units), a Monterey for 1961 (when series were shuffled and Park Lane axed, 7000 built), and a Monterey Custom for '62 (around 5500). A "1962½" entry was the Monterey Custom S-55, priced $500 above the standard convertible ($3738) and much like it apart from buckets, console, and other sporty features then coming into vogue. Only 1315 were built, though. The completely restyled '63 ($3900) saw only 64 more.

The Park Lane and its convertible returned for '64 (Mercury's silver anniversary year), complementing a $3226 soft top in that season's base-line Monterey series. Neither was numerous: 1967 and 2592 units, respectively. But vol-

Chevy's 1964 Impala SS convertible (*above left*) was yours for $3196. At the other end of the spectrum was the '64 Imperial drop-top (*above*), priced at a sobering $6003. Ford's 1964 Falcon Futura Sprint (*below left*) flew with a standard 260-cid V-8. The '64 Ford Galaxie 500/XL (*below right*) offered a 425-bhp V-8.

ume improved for '65, when the big Mercs were restyled *à la* Lincoln and touted as "fine cars in the Continental tradition." The ragtop Monterey garnered 4762 orders, the Park Lane 6853. For '66, the S-55 returned as a separate series. Its convertible, priced at a reasonable $3614, saw only 669 copies. Demoted to a Monterey subseries the following year, S-55 scored only 145 convertibles, then was canned.

Meantime, the soft top 1967 Park Lane was down to 1191 units, the Monterey to 2673. After equally low numbers of '68s, the full-size Mercs were all-new for '69, when Marquis ousted Park Lane as the top-line series. A convertible continued there (a handsome beast and more Lincoln-like than ever), but volume didn't improve much, totaling 2319. The standard Monterey model was still around, though barely at just 1297 units. Mercury would continue big convertibles through 1971, then give up.

The Comet, Mercury's compact, received its first convertibles for 1963, at the same time that the Ford Falcon offered its first ragtop model. Bench-seat Custom and bucket-seat S-22 models, offered at $2557/$2710, racked up over 13,000 sales between them, a big part of Mer-

Ford's Thunderbird gained new, squarer lines for 1964 (*above left*). The '64 Oldsmobile Starfire ragtop (*above*) ran with a 345-bhp 394-cid V-8. Pontiac sold speed by stuffing a 389-cid V-8 into an intermediate chassis to make the '64 GTO (*below left*). Studebaker's final ragtop was the '64 Daytona (*below right*).

cury's 1963 ragtop record. After the 1962-63 Meteor failed to make the hoped-for impression in the mid-size field, Comet was elongated and embellished to fill in. A lone convertible was available for 1964-65, in the second-from-top Caliente series, priced around $2650 and good for just over 15,000 units a year.

For 1966, Comet became a true intermediate and offered three convertibles: the Caliente, plus base and GT models in that year's newly expanded high-performance Cyclone series. The latter was Mercury's rival to the likes of the Pontiac GTO, Olds 4-4-2, and Dodge Coronet R/T. Powered by Ford's 335-bhp 390 V-8, the Cyclone offered a variety of useful suspension options. The '67 was even more exciting with its new 427 option. Similar street racers were available among the all-new 1968 models—but not as convertibles, as the Cyclones and Caliente were dropped in favor of a single offering in that year's new luxury Montego MX series; it lasted just a single season. None of these mid-size Merc droptops sold more than about 2000 units a year except for the '66 Caliente (3922) and '68 Montego (3248).

Mercury was late in getting a version of the Mustang, but its new-for-'67 Cougar was smashing: longer and more luxurious than the Ford, identified by an "electric shaver" grille and sequential rear turn signals. Convertibles had to wait until 1969, when Cougar became longer and wider, somewhat fussier in appearance, and adopted

ventless side glass. Like the original hardtop, the open Cougar came in plain-vanilla and XR-7 guise, the latter with rich leather seat trim and comprehensive instrumentation surrounded by simulated walnut. Production came to about 6000 standards and 4000 XR7s. Perhaps reflecting Mercury's growing diffidence toward convertibles, the hottest '69 Cougar, the new Eliminator, was offered only as a hardtop.

At Ford Division, general manager Lee Iacocca approved the Thunderbird Sports Roadster for 1962 in hopes of satisfying public clamor for a new two-seater. Designer Bud Kaufman came up with a fiberglass tonneau to cover the normal convertible's back-seat area, giving it faired-in headrests for the front buckets. He also overcame fitting problems so that the top could be raised or lowered with the cover in place. Kelsey-Hayes wire wheels were standard, and the stock rear fender skirts were left off to accommodate them.

The result was striking, but at a hefty $5439—$650 more than the regular T-Bird convertible—the Sports Roadster attracted only 1427 buyers for the '62 and 455 for the near-identical '63. The model was duly canceled for

'64, though a similar tonneau became a dealer option for the regular convertible. (Few were sold.) Topless T-Bird demand peaked that year, then declined rapidly. Model-year 1966 thus saw the last of the flock, 5049 in all. For 1967, the hardtop was enlarged and an even larger four-door sedan added, beginning the "big 'Bird" era.

Mustang was a far more successful idea (one generally, though not accurately, ascribed to Iacocca). It took Detroit by storm with record first-year sales for a new model: 680,000 from its April 1964 introduction through the end of model-year '65. Built to a price (about $2500 base) using off-the-shelf components, Mustang succeeded by dint of pretty, long-hood/short-deck styling and a myriad of options by which customers could make it anything from economy compact to road-burning grand tourer.

For once, a convertible generated serious volume: 101,945 units in Mustang's first, extra-long model year—15 percent of total production. The topless Mustang, in fact, was a big reason for the industry's record soft top sales in '65. Yet this initial flood seemed to satiate demand. By 1967, the convertible was the slowest-selling of Mustang's three body styles, then dropped to fewer than 15,000 units two years later.

A similar fate awaited Ford's other convertibles. The division entered the decade with a handful, had eight by 1966, then slimmed to six by 1970. Four years later there'd be none, though the convertible Mustang would be back.

Falcon was the biggest smash of the Big Three's original 1960 compacts: cleanly styled, cheap, reliable, and simple. Like Corvair and Valiant, it soon moved slightly upmarket with the help of folding-top models, but Falcon's wouldn't last long: introduced as a bucket-seat Futura for 1963, then dropped for '66 in deference to the Mustang convertible. There was also a Futura Sprint companion, a mid-1963 addition with standard buckets-and-console interior, tachometer, and Falcon's first V-8 option: the smooth, potent 260-cid small-block, upgraded with more horsepower for '65 as the 289. Production was unusually modest—4602 of the '63s, 4278 of the '64s, 300 of the '65s—so the Sprint convertibles are by the far the most collectible Falcons.

Ford's full-size Sunliner continued throughout the decade in the top-line series: Galaxie for 1960-61, Galaxie 500 thereafter. Bucket-seat 500/XL versions were available from "1962 ½," renamed plain XL for 1969. The posh LTD, a new Galaxie subseries for '65 and top of the line

The fierce-looking 1965 Buick Wildcat (*above*) offered a 425-cid V-8. Rambler fielded a full line of convertibles for the first time in 1965; the Classic 770 (*right*) went for $2696. The '65 Mustang (*far right*) turned into a gold mine for Ford. Buyers could order from an expansive menu of options; in all, first-year Mustang production totaled 101,945.

thereafter, wasn't offered as a ragtop until 1966, and then only for a year, when a lush "7-Litre" sub-model appeared with standard 428 big-block V-8. Just 2368 were built.

The intermediate Fairlane, new for '62, was another Ford hit, if a somewhat smaller one than Falcon and Mustang. Convertibles weren't available until the enlarged second generation of 1966-67, when Fairlane 500, 500/XL, and XL GT models appeared, the last with standard 390 V-8 or, less typically, the muscular 427. The mid-size Fords were completely redesigned for '68, becoming a bit larger and heavier and gaining curvier "Coke-bottle" styling. Ragtops were down to two: a $2822 bench-seat Fairlane 500 and a $3001 bucket-seat GT in the new upper-crust Torino series. Fairlane convertible assemblies usually numbered 4000-6000 a year, though some individual models saw fewer. The '67 500/XL, for instance, ran to just 1943 examples, the GT to 2117, the '69 Torino GT to 2552.

General Motors was the company with the most to lose from the convertible's steady sales slide in the late Sixties. Four of its five divisions invariably figured among the top five convertible producers, and the fifth, Cadillac, was never far behind. For 1965, the year Detroit built half a million ragtops, GM contributed over 300,000, and well over a third were of those were Chevrolets.

One reason was Corvette, which fielded the stunning Sting Ray for 1963 as an alternative to the customary "roadster." Helped by a $200-$300 price advantage, convertible 'Vettes handily outsold coupes through 1968. Then the coupe took hold, not least because it became a semi-open style—the first "T-top," in fact—offering much of the roadster's open-air feel without its usual drawbacks.

Corvette volume passed 10,000 for the first time with the 1960 models, little-changed from the '59s. GM design chief Bill Mitchell gave the '61s a handsome new "duck-tail," while the touched-up '62s introduced the 327-cid small-block that would be Corvette's mainstay V-8 through 1965.

Then came the Sting Ray, with exciting Mitchell styling on a four-inch shorter wheelbase (98 inches) and Corvette's first independent rear suspension, engineered by Zora Arkus-Duntov. Sales broke 20,000 units that season, and continued upward each year except for a modest decline in '67. Styling progressively improved too, and

Optional with the 1965 Dodge Dart GT (*top left*) was a 273-cid 180-bhp V-8. The handsome '65 Lincoln Continental (*left*) rang up sales of 3356. Coronet (*above, top*) bowed as Dodge's mid-size entry for 1965. The largest Dodge convertible for 1965 was the Custom 880 (*above, middle*), which came with a 383-cid V-8. Top of the line at Olds for '65 was the $4493 98 (*above*).

Squared-off styling introduced for 1965 continued on Cadillac for '66 (*top*). Chevy's '66 Impala (*above*) started at $3041. Mustang's popularity continued to run high for 1966 (*right*), with 72,119 examples sold. The Olds 4-4-2 (*below*) became a separate model for '66, and gave potent performance via a 400-cid 350-bhp V-8. And muscle was flexing at Pontiac, as well, thanks to the '66 GTO (*below right*) and its standard 333-bhp 389.

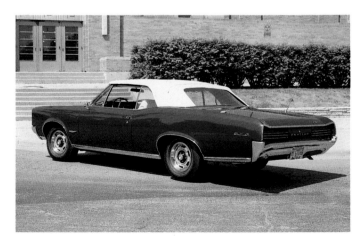

performance got a big boost from big-block V-8s beginning in '65, the last year for fuel injection and the first for disc brakes.

Corvette was rebodied for '68, becoming bigger, brasher, and more begadgeted. Many observers decried all of that, as well as sloppy workmanship, but there were more buyers than ever: close to 40,000 for the '69s. By that point, the open Corvette started at $4438, up from 1960's $3872 base price.

Not quite as sporty, but at least of temporary importance in the soft top picture, was Chevy's rear-engine Corvair. Open models were first offered for '62 in Monza and new turbocharged Monza Spyder form. The pair garnered a healthy 44,000 sales the following year. Model-years 1965-69 brought the last open Corvairs: Monza and, through 1966, a new uplevel Corsa model with optional turbo-power. The latter ran to 8353 and 3142 units for 1965-66, respectively. Monza began at around 26,500, plummeted by over half for '66 and sank to 1386 units two years later.

Ultimately, keen competition from the Mustang and public concern over alleged handling defects kneecapped the Corvair; by 1969, sales of the open Monza were a puny 521.

Other Chevy model lines were equally replete with convertibles. The full-size Impala series offered a standard bench-seat model throughout the decade, plus a sporty SS variant for 1962-67 (it reverted to option status for 1968-69). A similar arrangement prevailed in the 1962-63 Chevy II line, which arrived as the economy compact Corvair had failed to be. The Chevy II Nova and SS ragtops were dropped when the intermediate Chevelle debuted for 1964 with two convertibles: Malibu and bucket-seat Malibu SS with choice of six or V-8.

Then came Camaro, taking careful aim at Mustang beginning with model-year '67. A convertible was part of its arsenal from the first. A few received the potent Z-28 engine/suspension package that won the Trans-Am Championship for Chevy in 1968-69. A sprightly performer with a wide range of V-8s and other options, the Camaro tallied upwards of a quarter-million annual sales in its early years and soon overtook Mustang. Convertibles accounted for as small a portion of Camaro's sales as they did Mustang's, and so the second-generation design announced for "1970½" appeared as a coupe only.

GM's number-two convertible outfit—and after 1967, number two in the industry—was Pontiac, riding high on the sporty image established when Bunkie Knudsen became division general manager back in '57. Pontiac's commitment to the convertible market was enormous: full-size Catalina and Bonneville; compact and mid-size Tempest, Tempest Le Mans and GTO; the Catalina-based 1966 2+2 and '67 Grand Prix (the latter a one-year-only version of Pontiac's big personal-luxury car with just 5876 built); and the Camaro-clone 1967-69 Firebird.

The legendary GTO was undoubtedly Pontiac's greatest Sixties convertible. It was introduced in mid-1964 and, unlike many others of its ilk, was offered as a convertible from day one. To order a '64 GTO convertible, the buyer began with a $2641 Tempest Custom or $2796 Tempest Le Mans droptop, then plunked down an extra $300 for the GTO package, which included 389 V-8, quick steering,

The capacious '67 Cadillac DeVille convertible (*top*) found 18,202 buyers at $5605. Chevrolet introduced its sporty Camaro for 1967 (*second from top*) and immediately won a loyal following. The restyled '67 Plymouth Barracuda (*third from top*) looked nice but paled next to the potent '67 Pontiac GTO (*above*).

Chrysler's 1965 300 (*top*) cost $4289 and came standard with a 350-bhp 440 V-8. Bargain-hunters appreciated the '65 Coronet line, which included Dodge's least expensive ($3036) convertible (*above*), available with an optional 383-cid V-8. Mercury's massive '65 Park Lane (*above right*) was nearly as big as a rec room, and could look like one, too, thanks to wood-plank decals. Pontiac's drop-top land yacht for '68 was the Bonneville (*right*), priced at $3800.

stiff shocks, dual exhausts, and premium tires. A four-speed manual gearbox cost $188, while sintered metallic brake linings, H. D. radiator, and limited-slip differential added $75. Another $115 bought a 360-bhp 389; by that point, all the new owner needed was a lead foot and lots of gas.

Oldsmobile and Buick, while not at Pontiac's volume, continued to produce lots of topless cars throughout the Sixties. Oldsmobile consistently offered one in each of its model lines, from compact F-85/Cutlass to full-size 98. There was also a special Super/Delta 88 ragtop in 1961-66, the buckets-and-console Starfire. Its annual volume ranged from 2236 (1965) to 13,019 (1966), with 4000 or 7000 in most years.

Olds' answer to GTO was the 4-4-2, introduced as an option package at mid-'64, then made a separate model from 1966. A convertible was available each year. The designation originally denoted four-speed gearbox, four-barrel carb, and dual exhausts; a 400 V-8 replaced the initial 330 for '65 and was factored into the model name. The 4-4-2 package cost only about $250 that year, a bargain. Included were special road wheels; heavy-duty springs and shocks; beefed-up rear axle, driveshaft, and engine mounts; special frame and steering ratio; stabilizer bars front and rear; fat tires; 11-inch-diameter clutch; 70-amp battery and special trim. Performance was on the order of 7.5 seconds 0-60 mph, the quarter-mile in 17 seconds at 85 mph.

Buick's most memorable Sixties soft tops were the Gran Sport and Wildcat. The latter began in 1962 as a special Invicta hardtop. A convertible and hardtop sedan were added the next year; Wildcat then replaced Invicta for '64. Most Wildcats had bucket seats, and all were offered with brawny V-8s that ran to a 325-bhp 401. The GS, a sporty Special/Skylark evolution, also began as a trim package, for '66, and became a separate series for '68.

Buick's biggest engine ever arrived for 1967: a new 430 V-8, standard on Wildcat, Electra, and the svelte Riviera personal-luxury coupe. It had little more horsepower than the 401, but was quieter and smoother-running. Also new was a 400 for intermediates, appearing on a GS400 convertible and hardtop coupe; the open version started near $3200.

Cadillac finished fifth or sixth in convertibles each year, underlining its traditional high appeal to moneyed luxury-minded buyers. This didn't require much model diversity, either. Through 1966, Cadillac got by with one Series 62/DeVille convertible at around $6000 and an upmarket Eldorado Biarritz some $1000 higher. The latter vanished for '67, when Eldorado was reborn as a front-drive coupe, but the soft top DeVille continued to account for about 17,000 sales each model year. This made Cadillac a major convertible producer, its volume exceeded only by that of ostensibly more popular makes like Plymouth, Dodge, and Mercury.

Studebaker aside, the Sixties ended with the same automakers as had started the decade. For the convertible, however, it was a topsy-turvy 10 years. In 1969, just four years after scoring record production, convertibles barely made it over the 200,000 mark, and changes in model lineups and body production for 1970 suggested that their ranks would be thinner still in years to come.

Chevy's last Camaro convertible for 18 years showed up in 1969 (*top*); this is an SS. The '69 Impala SS (*middle*) could be had with a hairy 427-cid 425-bhp V-8. The first Mercury Cougar convertibles, including an XR7 model (*above*), bowed for 1969.

65

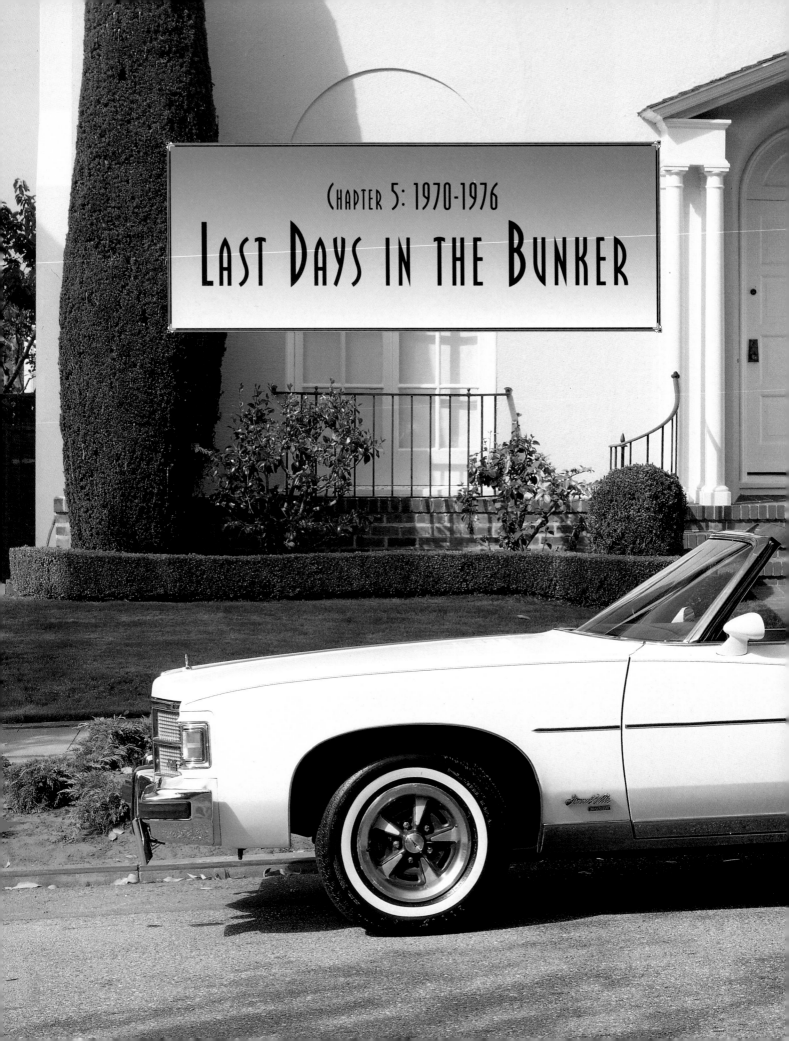

CHAPTER 5: 1970-1976
LAST DAYS IN THE BUNKER

The good looks of this '75 Pontiac Grand
Ville notwithstanding, American convertibles
were extinct by 1976.

What killed the American convertible in the mid-Seventies?

When Cadillac Motor Car Division announced that its 1976 Eldorado, by then America's sole production convertible, would be the last of its kind, "experts" rushed to explain why: Convertibles weren't safe; people were keenly aware of smog and no longer drove unnecessarily; jammed freeways and urban thoroughfares diminished the fun of driving. But the real reason for the ragtop's incipient demise was far simpler: a lack of sales.

Sales, that is, of domestic models. Technically, you see, the ragtop never really died in the U.S.—not with topless imports from VWs to Rolls-Royces, convertible conversions of domestic coupes (which began appearing even before that last '76 Eldo), and the Jeep CJ. And guess what? A new generation of American convertibles would be born in 1982, beginning with Lee Iacocca and Chrysler Corporation.

Still, the fact remains that American "factory" convertibles were absent nearly six years because they hadn't sold. But why hadn't they? Moreover, how could their sales plunge so drastically within five years of setting an all-time record?

Buick's 1970 LeSabre Custom (*top left*) came with a 350-cid 260-bhp V-8 that gave smart performance. The '70 Dodge Coronet R/T (*top right*), with optional hemi engine, sold just 296 copies. Chrysler's 1970 300 (*above*) came with 440 big-block power.

Some observers credited the two-door hardtop with the convertible's demise, reasoning that the former offered a sporty look but with apparent added safety.

A second factor came into play around 1955: affordable imports. Before the Volkswagen, whose sales first alarmed Detroit that year, foreign cars had been small potatoes in the vast U.S. market. But many had been convertibles or roadsters—Jaguars, MGs, Triumphs—and experience with all kinds of imports began increasing buyer dissatisfaction with Detroit cars. The ranks of these customers swelled dramatically in the Sixties and reached Herculean proportions by the mid-Seventies, which spelled big trouble for Detroit's market share in general and the convertible's in particular.

We should also not forget the tragedy of the American misadventure in Vietnam, which claimed 57,000 young American lives and maimed thousands more. It's likely that many would have bought convertibles, especially the muscle-car variety. And we all know that muscle cars withered as much as convertibles in 1965-75.

A final nail in the convertible's coffin was the simple march of technology: the advent and almost universal adoption of more efficient and affordable air conditioning systems; sealing, sound-isolation, and other body improvements that really *did* render closed cars far quieter and more comfortable than convertibles; and the arrival of sunroofs and moonroofs, which provided much of a convertible's feel with none of the inconvenience.

But enough sociology and on to the cars. Statistics tell a lot of the story:

YEAR	CONVERTIBLES	% OF MARKET
1965	509,419	5.48
1969	201,997	2.46
1970	91,863	1.40
1974	27,955	0.50

American Motors had abandoned convertibles after 1968. Chrysler Corporation followed suit after 1971, going from 11 to three in just one year.

Considering its future role in reviving them, the Chrysler marque's early abandoning of convertibles is ironic. The 1970 Newport and 300, on the 124-inch wheelbase used for all models that year except Town & Country wagons, would be the last Chrysler convertibles until 1982. Die-hards flocked to buy them, though too few. Only 1124 Newports and 1077 300s were built, all early in the model year.

As an artifact, the 300 is to be preferred today. It came with the big 440-cubic-inch V-8, offering 350/375 gross horsepower. Newports had a 383, with the 440 optional. The 300's base price was $4580 against $3925 for the Newport, but a low-mileage original 300 is now worth 50 percent more than a comparable Newport—and both bring more than what they cost new, albeit in inflated dollars.

Dodge and Plymouth opened the decade with more elaborate convertible programs that dissolved in a hurry. Dodge's 1970 line included five ragtops in three model groups. The new 110-inch-wheelbase Challenger ponycar and mid-size 117-inch Coronet 500 contained base and sportier R/T models (the latter offering a 440 option). The 122-inch-wheelbase Polara V-8, that year's base full-size Dodge, carried a $3500 convertible.

The R/Ts were probably over-engined, especially the Challenger, though they did have carefully tuned (if hard-riding) chassis to handle the big-block's power. And they remained the clean, speedy-looking Detroit-style grand tourers R/Ts had been in the Sixties. But the market just wasn't there. Dodge duly yanked all but the base Challenger convertible for '71.

Plymouth's convertibles paralleled Dodge's except for an additional version of the hulkier, heavier new 1970 Barracuda. The Challenger, of course, was Dodge's belated ponycar, planned alongside the third-generation Barracuda but aimed more at Mercury Cougar than Ford Mustang. Both arrived for 1970 sharing basic underbody structure, chassis, and drivetrains, though the Dodge rode a two-inch longer wheelbase (110 inches) and differed in some styling elements. Both tailed off to just two closed models for 1973-74, then vanished.

The $3501 1970 Ford Galaxie 500/XL (*top*) brought a standard 351-cid V-8. Mustang (*second from top*) saw convertible sales for '70 drop to 7673—half the level of 1969. But the '70 Torino (*third from top*) sold better than in '69; a 220-bhp 302 was standard. Plymouth's '70 Barracuda (*above*) offered a 383-cid V-8 rated at 335 bhp.

Like Challenger, the third-generation Barracuda took a "more ponycar" approach to a market that was still strong at the time development work commenced. The new design feature for both was a provision for big-block engines, up to and including the jumbo 440 and fiery 425-horsepower street hemi. So equipped, the ragtops made a play to be the fastest of Detroit's 1970-71 herd.

The 1970 Barracudas comprised hardtop and convertible in standard, luxury Gran Coupe, and performance-oriented 'Cuda trim—meaning that, yes, you could buy a "Gran Coupe convertible," though only in 1970. Ragtop prices that year ran $3034 to $3433. The standard cars came with a six; Gran Coupes carried the venerable 318 V-8 as standard, the muscle-laden 'Cudas a 383.

Like Dodge, Plymouth reprised standard and sporty intermediate convertibles and one full-size model for 1970. Respectively, these were Satellite, Road Runner, and Fury III. The mid-size GTX and big Sport Fury models did not return from '69. The Satellite name had replaced Belvedere on Plymouth intermediates for '68, the year Road Runner was introduced. The '70 line marked the last of this mid-size generation—and mid-size Plymouth ragtops.

All of which makes the 1970 RR convertible a highly desirable collector's item today. Named for the popular Warner Bros. cartoon character, the Runner still came with cartoon decals and "beep-beep" horn. As before, the '70 lived up to that name: Tightly sprung, it cornered as if on rails and accelerated like an artillery shell when it had to (which was most of the time for many owners). V-8s

Because a Dodge Challenger paced the Indy 500 in 1971, 50 pace-car replicas (*top left*) were produced for pre-race activities. The unhappy expansion of the Mercury Cougar's girth continued for '71 (*top right*); sales of combined base and ragtop Cougars totaled a modest 3440. The end for the Olds 4-4-2 came in '71 (*above left and right*), after which the car reverted to option status.

were the same stalwart array 'Cudas offered, including the street hemi.

But 1972's swoopy new-generation design gave Chrysler a convenient excuse for forgetting mid-size Dodge and Plymouth convertibles, hence their termination. As a hardtop, the Road Runner would survive through 1975. Then Chrysler abandoned performance cars across the board and the Runner became a "paint-on performance" version of the compact Volare—about which the less said, the better.

The Fury III was Plymouth's best-selling soft top in these years, the top of the full-size line ($3415 for 1970) other than the hardtop Sport Fury GT and exotic Superbird. But it was all relative: Plymouth convertible volume shrunk just like Dodge's, going from 1554 for the 1970 Barracuda to a microscopic 374 for the '71 'Cuda. Other models fared little better.

For Ford Motor Company, it was, as the philosopher said, a case of "the same story, only more so." The convertible took longer to die at Dearborn, but the handwriting was on the wall. Lincoln had given up after 1967; Mercury averaged about 4000 a year in 1970-73, Ford about 13,000. By that point, the only ones left were Mustang and Cougar. Both were scrubbed for '74, when Cougar became

a fat-cat intermediate and the original ponycar was replaced by the underwhelming Mustang II.

The end of the droptop Mustang seemed inconceivable, for the convertible had been a big part of Mustang's early success. Though it found fewer buyers as the years passed, it was always there, touted with let-them-eat-cake praise and prominent in the brochures. Maybe it doesn't sell, Ford seemed to be saying, but it sure helps Mustang's image.

And Ford product planners gave the convertible their best possible shot. Unlike Chrysler and GM rivals, the topless Mustang was never diluted by sub-models. There was always just one, albeit with the usual long list of options, including wild engines. And it did have a following, a much larger one than for other roofless ponycars. When Ford announced that the 1973 Mustang ragtop would be the last, dealers moved close to 12,000, 50 percent more than the annual total for 1970-72.

Ford's other convertibles were a prosaic lot, few in number, and sooner extinct. The intermediate Torino, restyled for 1970 into one of Dearborn's ugliest cars ever, offered its last soft top for '71, a GT model (1613 sold). The full-size Ford did better, recording 6348 XL sales for 1970 and 5750/4234 for 1971-72, when it finally shifted to the top-line $4500-$5000+ LTD series.

Predictably, Mercury still mostly followed Ford's convertible strategy. An exception was the continuation of standard and XR-7 Cougars for 1970-73. Priced about $500 above the soft top Mustang, they still aimed at better-heeled types. Trouble was, few such buyers seemed to

want convertibles now. Though much larger and heavier than the original, these Cougars were nice-looking, well-appointed cars—and quick when equipped with one of the 351 or 428 V-8s—but 4000 units a year was hardly impressive volume for an outfit like Lincoln-Mercury.

Unlike Ford, Mercury gave up on mid-size droptops after 1969. Its only other offerings were gigantic, 124-inch-wheelbase Monterey and Marquis models that respectively garnered 581 and 1233 sales for 1970, their final year.

The sheer size and product spread of General Motors virtually assured that the world's largest automaker would field the most convertibles of the Big Three and stay with them the longest. But even GM couldn't escape the market's turn from topless motoring. Its offerings thus dwindled from 18 different 1970 models to six by '73. Three years later, the Cadillac Eldorado would be the only droptop Detroiter left.

The Chevrolet Corvette convertible persisted through 1975, though the companion T-top coupe had surpassed it in sales in 1969 and took an increasing share of each subsequent year's pie. The final edition saw only 4629 convertibles, the lowest production for an open Corvette since 1956. Interestingly, Corvette performance took a dive at the same time. For 1970, a new 454-cid enlargement of Chevy's big-block V-8, designed to better meet emissions standards, replaced the previously optional 427s. But the most powerful (465-bhp) version planned was never offered because it couldn't be cleaned up enough to satisfy federal guidelines. For the same reason, the solid-lifter 350 LT-1 small-block option bit the dust after 1970.

Such changes took big bites out of Corvette's top power ratings: 460 bhp for 1970, 425 for '71, 270 for '72, an anemic 205 (SAE net) by 1975. This plus new federally mandated safety equipment made a change in the car's character inevitable. By 1975, Corvette had become a more balanced car—less outlandish, arguably more pleasant to drive—a plush high-speed GT instead of a stark straight-line screamer. Continued strong sales seemed to bear out the wisdom of these changes.

There were two others: the Chevy Camaro Z-28 and Pontiac's Firebird Trans Am. But both these ponycars were out of the ragtop field by virtue of Bill Mitchell's coupe-only second generation of 1970.

Little topless material appeared in Chevy's other model lines. Through 1972 it consisted of a mid-size Chevelle Malibu and full-size Impala, base-priced at about $3200 and $4000, respectively, but selling for more like $4000/$5000 with popular options. The hot Malibu Super Sport was now an option package, but could be ordered with either the 454, pumping out 425 gross bhp for '71, or a 402-cid, 300-bhp V-8 evolved from the original 396 (and still called that).

GM switched all intermediates to new "Colonnade" styling for 1973, which meant pillared instead of pillarless hardtop coupes and sedans—and no more convertibles. Not counting the Corvette, this left Chevy with just the big convertible, built on the corporate B-body platform with a grand 121.5-inch wheelbase. Reasoning that it

might as well shoot for the maximum buck, the division duly spruced up the Impala convertible into a Caprice Classic for 1973. It lasted only three model years.

Though it cost a lot—$4400-$4800 base, some $500-$800 up on the previous Impala—this Caprice was a nice car: roomy, luxurious, a smooth cruiser—and a dinosaur rapidly heading for the automotive tar pits. (In the wake of the 1973-74 fuel crisis, GM had decided to downsize its big cars, the first of which would appear, *sans* convertibles, for 1977.) But people liked it about as much as any convertible in those days, especially once they heard it was going away. The last-of-the-line '75 sold 8339 copies, the highest figure for any Seventies Chevrolet convertible.

Through 1974, Chevrolet continued to lead the industry in convertible volume, stunted though that had become. But with the end of intermediate and ponycar soft tops, "USA-1" was overtaken in 1975 by Oldsmobile, which had been running a close second. In fact, Olds built nearly half of all Detroit's 1975 ragtops and almost twice as many as Chevrolet. You could say that Lansing was among the final holdouts during the convertible's "last days in the bunker."

There was a reason for this, though only one: Olds had made a conscious effort to mop up most of whatever convertible market remained by mid-decade. By that point it had just one mop, a topless Delta 88 Royale, $5200 of full-size, 124-inch-wheelbase luxury cruiser that weighed in at a portly 4300 pounds. The convertible offered a healthy helping of standard features: power steering and front

Total Mustang convertible production for 1972 was 6401, and included this patriotically themed ragtop with the optional "Sprint" decor package (*below*).

disc brakes, deluxe steering wheel, steel-belted radial tires, and a 170-bhp (SAE net) 350 V-8. Styling after '72 suffered mainly from the clunky 5-mph bumpers found on most big Detroit cars at the time—which gave it the prow of an 18-wheeler.

The Delta Royale was Olds's only convertible after 1972, but sales had been miserable until '75. All the publicity surrounding it (more, in fact, than attended the Caprice) allowed the last topless Olds to go out a modest success.

Royale aside, few other Olds ragtops survived past 1970. That year saw the last big Ninety-Eight. The next saw the end of the once-popular 4-4-2 muscle car, which reverted to option status for 1972. Like all others, 4-4-2 convertible numbers were low: 2933 of the '70s, 1304 of the '71s. The soft top mid-size Cutlass, offered from 1970 only as a bucks-up Supreme model, said *adieu* after '72, though it managed a respectable 11,000-plus sales that year. Overall, Oldsmobile gave a dying breed one of its best shots, building well over 80,000 convertibles in 1970-75, second only to Chevrolet.

Buick and Pontiac turned in almost identical performances in the Seventies. Each division built about 15,000 convertibles for 1970, the last significant production year, about 8000 for 1971 and '72, and about half that number for 1973-75.

Five convertibles returned in the 1970 Buick line: the traditional LeSabre/Wildcat/Electra trio, still on enormous 124- and 127-inch wheelbases, and the intermediate Skylark Custom and Gran Sport, the latter mounting a standard 455-cid V-8 with 350/360 bhp. Wildcat (1244 built) and GS 455 (1416) were the rarest, which naturally makes them the most collectible today.

The 455 was a kind of valedictory to the age of big-inch engines. Buick's largest ever, it had a compression ratio of at least 10:1 and returned only 10-12 miles per gallon of premium gas. The most powerful version was also used in 1970's senior Electra 225 series, which included the last Electra convertible.

Minus that one, Buick's ragtops repeated for '71, except that the Wildcat series was renamed Centurion. Convertible sales were broadly lower, the Gran Sport sinking to 902 units, for example. With 1973's "Colonnade" intermediates and cancellation of the ragtop LeSabre, the Centurion was Buick's sole convertible. Then that series was dropped and the convertible became a LeSabre again, offered only in upmarket Custom trim. It, too, would depart after 1975, when production totaled 5300.

Like their divisional counterparts, the big '71 Buicks were as large as American cars would ever get. More rounded styling marked that year's new B/C-body design, with "fuselage" sides, massive hoods, and broad expanses of glass. GM's full-sizers continued in this form through 1976, with mainly minor annual changes to meet safety and emissions requirements. Then all were downsized, the first phase of a corporate-wide "big shrink" that was accompanied by a growing uniformity among GM's cars, reflected in its "last" convertibles of the Seventies. Strict market separation, the guiding principle of Al Sloan, had been sacrificed during the expansive Sixties in

Cadillac offered an Eldo convertible for 1972 (*below left*), at $7546. Chevy's Impala convertible (*below right*), with standard V-8, sold for $3979. The '72 Hurst Olds pace-car replica (*bottom left*) commemorated Olds's involvement in that year's Indy 500. Ford's "upscale" LTD badge offered a drop-top for '72 (*bottom right*).

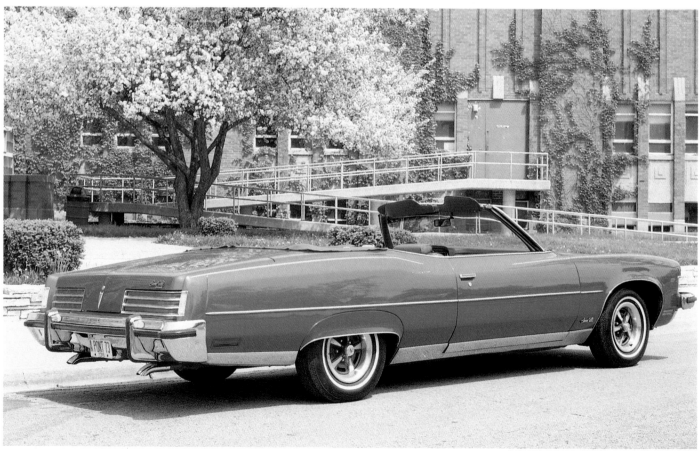

favor of platforms (in the necessary sizes) shared by as many divisions as possible. To some extent, this was prompted by demands from each dealer group for as many different kinds of cars as possible. But when the market contracted in the early Seventies, GM found itself with too many look-alike, overlapping model lines spread among five makes whose identities were no longer so clear to customers. The similarities began to hurt.

Nowhere was this more apparent than at Pontiac, which mainly marketed the same cars as Buick, Olds, and Chevrolet. (Only the names were changed to protect division executives.) Its convertibles thus followed the same pattern. For the record, Pontiac sold full-size soft tops as a Catalina (1970-72), Bonneville (1970), and Grand Ville (1971-75). Typical yearly production was around 3000-4500 units except 1971-72, when the Catalina and Grand Ville saw fewer than 2500 each.

Also like sister divisions, Pontiac lost its mid-size convertibles with the 1973 "Colonnade" generation. It was just as well, as Pontiac could sell no more than 6000 of any one model in 1970-72. This made for some rather rare rag-

tops. For instance, the 1971 GTO managed only 661 convertibles, while that year's flashy, high-performance GTO Judge saw exactly 17.

Under division chief John Z. DeLorean, who claimed never to have made a mistake, Pontiac policy had been to outflank Chevy in the low-price field while challenging Olds/Buick in the medium-price ranks. But the results were an untimely blurring of Pontiac's "with it" image, a slide in assembly quality, a pile-up of unsold cars, and sales losses to Oldsmobile and Buick. In fact, Olds nosed out Pontiac in 1973 model-year registrations, the first time that had happened since 1958; by 1975, both Olds and Buick were threatening Pontiac's number-three spot. And while Pontiac had usually run fifth in convertible volume, Cadillac surpassed it in 1973.

The '75 Buick LeSabre convertible (*top*) sold 5300 units at $5133—a creditable performance that was doubtless inspired by buyer interest in the car's status as the "last" of the Buick ragtops. The price of an Eldorado convertible (*above*) topped 10 grand for 1975—a cool $10,354. Sales of 8950 weren't bad at all, but were just a foretaste of the Eldo figures that would come a year later. The '75 Olds Delta 88 Royale convertible (*right*) cost $5200 and found 21,038 buyers.

Cadillac wasn't much affected by such intramural battles. Above the fray in its traditional luxury sector, it continued with a quarter-million or more annual sales in the early Seventies—and to make money with just one convertible. The 1970 model was still a 130-inch-wheelbase DeVille, priced at $6068 that year. Then, with 1971's new C-body, the DeVille was replaced by a soft top version of the front-drive Eldorado, itself redesigned and grossly enlarged that year. At $7751, the revived Eldo convertible (the first since '66) wrung more profit from fewer sales. A good thing, as yearly production hovered around 7500, versus 30,000-40,000 coupes. Nevertheless, as convertibles from other makes vanished, the Eldo came to be a prestige item for Cadillac; one even paced the 1973 Indianapolis 500.

But the deck was stacked against it almost from the first. For 1972, the Eldo hardtop appeared with a new "Custom Cabriolet" option, which meant an electric-sliding steel sunroof over the front seats and an elk-grain-vinyl rear half-roof (complete with "halo" trim molding). The more convenient sunroof, of course, was one of the key developments that hastened the droptop's demise.

A feature dating back to the original 1953 Eldorado appeared on the '72 convertible: a metal boot or tonneau over the top well. Electronic fuel injection was optional by 1975, when Cadillac proffered another anti-convertible idea: the Astro Roof, a tinted-glass power moonroof with sliding interior sunshade.

The funeral notices for the American convertible were prompted by Cadillac's announcement that the '76 Eldorado convertible would be the last. The division even announced production in advance: 14,000—up nearly 60 percent on the '75 total. While that represented the number of convertible tops and mechanisms left in stock, Cadillac was clearly milking this "milestone" for all its worth.

Gripped by last-chance acquisitiveness, buyers beat down the doors—and, figuratively, each other sometimes. In the end, Cadillac Division chose to single out the last *200*. All were painted white and had white tops, wheel covers, and upholstery, plus a special dash plaque attesting to "the end of an era."

The '76 Eldorado convertibles, the last 200 in particular, thus became the subjects of a remarkable con job perpetrated by dealers and quick-thinking speculators. Would-be owners began offering well over sticker, which was about $12,000, thus sending delivered prices toward the moon. Dealers, meantime, had naturally stocked up against the expected onslaught of these suckers. Ignorant "money" magazines, the more ignorant general media, and even the National Automobile Dealers Association *Used Car Guide* touted '76 values well above those for the '75s—as much as *eight years* after they were built.

Unheard in this near hysteria were the voices of experienced car collectors and organizations like the Cadillac-LaSalle Club and Milestone Car Society. The '76 Eldorado convertible, they warned, was about 50 percent more common than the '75; ready-made collector's items are rarely good investments; and new convertibles were still being built if one cared to count AMC's Jeeps or the imports.

But buyers didn't listen, of course, some paying up to $30,000 for one of these "last convertibles"—proving once again that P. T. Barnum was right. Today, a '76 Eldo convertible is worth little, if any, more than a '75 in comparable condition.

Cadillac offered a convertible again in 1984. Of course, by that time it wasn't alone. But that story, and the tale of the ragtop's rebirth throughout Detroit, deserves a chapter of its own.

Chapter 6: 1982-1989
New Beginnings

The 1983 Dodge 400 was just one reason convertible fanciers had reason to smile again in the Eighties.

After a six-year absence, the domestic droptop reappeared for 1982. The '82 Dodge 400 was hardly the summit of the convertible maker's art, but it did bode well for the future.

By 1980, automotive technology was catching up with the demands of government regulations. Chrysler was on the rebound (thanks to a fed/taxpayer bailout and some astute Chrysler management), and the horrors of gas shortages had begun to fade from memory. In essence, the auto industry was smarter and more robust, and for the first time in years, its future seemed bright.

In his best-selling autobiography, Chrysler's then-chief Lee Iacocca remembered, "In 1982, as we began to get healthy again, I decided to bring back the convertible. As an experiment, I had one built by hand from a Chrysler LeBaron. I drove it over the summer, and I felt like the Pied Piper. People in Mercedes and Cadillacs started running me off the road and pulling me over like a cop. 'What are you driving?' they all wanted to know. 'Who built it? Where can I get one?'"

Although Iacocca claimed that Chrysler subsequently plunged into convertible production without research, the decision to go ahead had almost certainly been made before his public drive. Also, Chrysler wasn't alone in the convertible's 1982 revival. That same year, Buick introduced a new soft top Riviera, the first ever, converted from Riv coupes by Detroit-based ASC Incorporated.

In any case, the domestic convertible was back. Propitiously introduced in time for the annual spring sales push (one of Iacocca's favored sales tactics when he was at Ford in the Sixties), Chrysler fielded a pair based on the new-for-'82 Chrysler LeBaron/Dodge 400. The first of many K-car variations to come, these were plusher, pricier, and slightly longer than Aries/Reliant but otherwise identical, riding the same 100.3-inch-wheelbase chassis. The ragtops came with the 2.6-liter Mitsubishi four optional on lesser models, and with its associated three-speed automatic transaxle.

Body shake and sluggish performance made the top-down behavior of these cars less than sterling, so the corporation set about making its ragtops more desirable. First came a new (mahogany-decaled) Town & Country model for '83, the first open T&C since 1949. Maintaining tradition, the new T&C was expensive—$16,300 initially—though that was almost exactly equivalent (in much-inflated dollars) to the '49 model's $3995. Newly optional for both ragtop LeBarons was a handsome Mark Cross package that included leather interior trim (unfortunately festooned with "MC" logos), cast-aluminum road wheels, more instruments (electronic, unfortunately)—yours for $2800.

The '84 LeBaron/400 convertibles featured a more compact top mechanism that liberated additional back-seat space, and new roll-down rear quarter windows that reduced the previous design's big over-the-shoulder blind spot. The backlight switched from plastic to glass. Dodge 400s became 600s for '85, by which time a new 600ES Turbo convertible was available with the blown, 147-horsepower version of Chrysler's own 2.2-liter four. A special sport/handling suspension package was standard, bringing larger front and rear anti-roll bars, "high-control" shocks, firmed-up power steering, and 60-series performance tires on "Swiss cheese" aluminum wheels. Base price was near $14,200.

For 1986, LeBaron and 600 were slightly restyled at each end and offered a second engine option: the new 2.5-liter version of Chrysler's "Trans-4," smoother than the base 2.2 by dint of a Mitsubishi-style balancer shaft. But then both these "CV-Series" convertibles were canceled for '87, leaving Dodge dealers with no ragtops and Chrysler-Plymouth stores with a handsome new LeBaron. For 1988, the Premium model was dressed up even further (automatic temperature controls, and such), and came in at $18,000. A less lavishly equipped "Highline" series was offered as a lower-priced alternative. Model-year 1989 brought a 2.5 turbo, and a GTC model equipped with an intercooled 2.2 turbo engine linked to a Getrag five-speed gearbox.

Also debuting in 1989 was the long-awaited TC, a two-seat convertible that was a joint effort between Chrysler and Maserati. This Italian-made hybrid offered no options, which made sense since each example, priced at $30,000, was loaded: leather interior, four-wheel anti-lock disc brakes, and removable hardtop. Engine choices comprised a 160-bhp intercooled 2.2 turbo with automatic and a Maserati 200-bhp 16-valve turbocharged and intercooled 2.2 with Getrag five-speed.

The TC was intended to be a limited-production item, but just how limited neither Chrysler nor Maserati could have known: The car's lofty price and indisputable resemblance to the far less exclusive LeBaron meant that fewer than 3000 TCs were sold during its debut year.

Chrysler's competitors did not sit on their hands while observing this convertible resurgence. Buick, as mentioned, fielded one for '82; Chevrolet and Ford jumped in for 1983; Pontiac and Cadillac in 1984. Still, Chrysler is generally credited with the ragtop revival—ironic, as it had never been able to sell that many in the old days.

Ford's "new generation" Mustang convertible, introduced in 1983, was successful, averaging about 20,000 sales annually throughout the decade. Intent upon stealing some of Chrysler's thunder, Ford first displayed its reborn convertible as a 1982 prototype, but didn't start production until the facelifted '83 Mustangs were ready. Bowing in top-line GLX trim at around $11,000, this new flip-top Ford featured roll-down rear side windows, stan-

Buick's 1983 Riviera convertible (*top*) carried an intimidating $24,960 price tag; only 1750 were sold. The first Mustang convertible since 1973 arrived for '83 (*above*), and found 23,438 buyers at $12,467 per copy. At Pontiac, the 2000 (*right*)—later known as the Sunbird—rang up 626 sales in its abbreviated first year.

dard power top, and glass backlight. As with other Mustangs, buyers could choose from normal and turbocharged 2.3-liter fours, 3.8 V-6, and the beloved 302-cubic-inch (4.9-liter) small-block V-8.

A rearranged '84 Mustang lineup presented three convertibles: base LX and two new GTs, V-8 and Turbo. The last, fussier to drive and costlier than the V-8 version, garnered few orders: a mere 600 or so that year (plus 2450 coupes). Exit Turbo GT.

All Mustangs got another nose job for '85, V-8 models another 25 horses. For '86, the 302 gained port fuel injection and a healthy 40 extra pounds/feet torque. Come 1987 and Mustang was again facelifted, in line with Ford's "aero" look; the V-6 option vanished. The '88s and '89s? Virtual reruns.

List price on the Mustang LX soft top had risen to just over $14,000 by 1989, while the GT remained a real performance bargain at about $17,000 base. The extra three grand bought the 225-bhp V-8, five-speed manual transmission, firm suspension, and limited-slip differential.

The ragtop Riviera, introduced almost simultaneously with Highland Park's first soft tops, was a logical step for the personal-luxury Buick. It was a good "image move" too, since Cadillac and Oldsmobile didn't immediately snip tops from their E-bodied Eldorado and Toronado. Yet the Riviera didn't sell, so it didn't last long, being dropped after model-year '85 (when production was only 400 units) after a total run of only about 4000 units. Per-

formance was not thrilling, and high price—$25,000 base, about $10,000 more than a comparable Riviera coupe—was another drawback.

What really killed the open Riviera was GM's switch to even-smaller new E-body cars for 1986. Buyers rebelled at the cars' high prices and styling that aped that of much cheaper GM models. It's doubtful that convertibles would have helped sales very much, as they would surely have cost more than the coupes. The official explanation for why the new Riv/Eldo/Toro had none was that a convertible conversion would have rendered the coupe's back seat unacceptably small. Fair enough, but GM had other plans, more of which will be discussed later.

Cadillac fielded a ragtop Eldo for 1984, offering it only in uplevel Biarritz trim. Like the Riv, it would vanish after '85. At $32,105 base, it was the most expensive U.S. production convertible ever built to that time, though price didn't kill it as much as the advent of that new E-body and the luxury market's continuing gravitation to imports.

83

Cadillac tried to stem the import tide—and polish up a quite tarnished image—with yet another, even costlier ($54,000 at announcement) convertible: the Allanté. Aimed at the more-expensive Mercedes 560SL, Cadillac's first modern-day production two-seater bowed with great fanfare for 1987 on a shortened (99.4-inch-wheelbase) Eldorado chassis with modified mechanicals. Power was supplied by the division's 4.1-liter transverse V-8 (as used in other front-drive Cadillacs through 1986) with multi-point (instead of single-point) fuel injection, roller valve lifters, high-flow cylinder heads, and tuned intake manifold providing 170 bhp.

The Allanté's tasteful but conservative styling came from Italy's renowned Pininfarina, which also built the bodywork and air-shipped it to Detroit from a new factory near Turin. Aluminum hood and trunklid were fixed to a galvanized unit-steel structure. Standard equipment was predictably complete, and included an SL-style lift-off hardtop to supplement the folding roof.

Though a capable tourer and an entirely new breed of Cadillac, the Allanté failed to make the hoped-for impression. Cadillac predicted 1987 model-year sales of 4000 units but got only 1651; for the first full production year, deliveries totaled just 2500 out of a planned 7000. Squeaks, wind noise, water leaks, oil leaks, and other problems turned off potential buyers. The result: an embarrassing pile-up of unsold cars, rebates to clear it—and a further blow to Cadillac's prestige.

After testing public reaction with a prototype, Chevy began selling the Cavalier convertible (converted by ASC Incorporated) in limited numbers beginning late in the '83 model year, when only 627 were built. But the ragtop was more readily available and in a greater variety of color and trim combinations for '84. It sold as a sporty Type-10 (which formerly meant only a hatchback coupe) at just over $11,000 base. All '84 Cavaliers were handsomely facelifted with quad headlamps, cross-hatch grille, and body-color bumpers. Subsequent facelifts and larger optional engines, including the fine 2.8-liter Chevy V-6, helped to broaden the ragtop Cavalier's appeal. By 1989, the convertible, by now called the Z-24, cost more than $16,500—a lot for a small car, even a competent ragtop.

Convertible fanciers were thrilled when Corvette (and ASC) brought back a convertible model for 1986—the first Corvette roadster in 11 years. Announced just in time to pace the Indy 500, it was based on the slightly smaller (96.2-inch-wheelbase) and lighter sixth-generation Corvette, introduced as a targa-top coupe in early 1983 for model-year '84. It naturally shared most of the coupe's pluses: sleek styling; sophisticated, all-independent suspension; powerful 350 V-8; and Bosch anti-lock braking system (from 1986). It also inherited most of the minuses: rocky ride, gimmicky electronic instruments, indifferent workmanship, and record prices—a little over $33,000 on introduction. Yet despite that, the reborn roadster (a misnomer; it remained a true convertible) sold well.

Left, from top: By 1986, the Chevy Cavalier ragtop could be had with a 2.0-liter four or 2.8-liter V-6; the Corvette convertible returned for 1986, as on this Indy pace-car replica; minor changes marked the '86 Chrysler LeBaron ragtop; the '86 Sunbird was available with a turbo option; AMC's entry into the convertible stakes was the Renault Alliance—this is an '86.

Successive model years brought added tweaks: added frame bracing for 1987; 245 horses for 1988, plus thicker all-disc brakes. Model-year 1989 brought a new six-speed manual gearbox and Selective Ride Control (the latter available only with manual transmission and the Z51 handling package), innovations that trickled down to "lesser" Corvette coupes and convertibles from the new ZR1 coupe, a mighty option package that brought a 32-valve, 385-bhp all-aluminum V-8.

Elsewhere at Chevy, the new Camaro convertible arrived in January 1987, sporting an ASC-rendered soft top that cheered dealers and enthusiasts alike. Another factory-approved conversion (by ASC), it was offered in the same four guises as that year's closed Camaro: high-performance IROC-Z and Z28, LT (Luxury Touring), and base V-6 Sport Coupe (was the last thus a "Sport Coupe convertible?"). Only 4000 were scheduled to be built that model year, all suitably reinforced to accommodate the soft top and engines that ran to the IROC's 5.7-liter, 220-bhp injected V-8. Base price was near $14,400, though a full-tilt IROC set buyers back another $3000 or more.

Although the LT and Z28 models were dropped for '88,

Cadillac struggled to regain lost prestige with the 1987 Allanté (*top*). Chevy's '87 IROC-Z Camaro (*above left*) strutted a 5.7-liter 220-bhp V-8. The redesigned '87 Chrysler LeBaron (*above middle*) sold briskly. Pontiac's turbo '87 Sunbird GT (*above right*) was priced at $15,569.

the remaining IROC and base models were cleanly styled and arguably the best-looking of the third-generation Camaros. For '89, the base model was given an RS tag along with swoopier bodywork. The IROC also took a step forward, offering Z-rated tires on 16-inch wheels and a 240-bhp version of the venerable 5.7-liter V-8.

Pontiac began offering ASC-converted soft top Sunbirds soon after the convertible Cavalier went on sale, but the Sunbird wouldn't have the Chevy's success. In 1986, for example, the Cav outsold the Bird 13 to three despite similar price tags, a rout that is at least partially due to the greater number and higher volume of Chevy dealerships.

First cataloged in the uplevel LE series for 1984, the Sunbird convertible was offered with the same three engines as other Sunbirds: Cavalier ohv four and normal and turbocharged versions of the new Opel-designed 1.8-liter overhead-cam four supplied to Pontiac (and Buick

Clockwise from top: Chevy's IROC-Z Camaro was little changed for '88; the '88 Corvette gained five more horses, to 245; Excalibur brought a neoclassic look to convertibles throughout the Eighties; a tweaked '88 Olds Cutlass Supreme paced the Indy 500 (note the '49 Olds in the background); Chevy sold 8745 Cavalier Z-24 ragtops for '88.

Chrysler aspired to prestige in 1989 with a hybrid car, the two-seat Chrysler's TC by Maserati. Shoppers were discouraged by a $30,000 price and a marked resemblance to the lesser LeBaron.

and Olds for their J-cars) by GM do Brasil. The LE became an SE for '86, when Pontiac added a new GT convertible with semi-hidden headlamps, rear spoiler, the turbo 1.8, and beefier Rally suspension. Both ohc engines grew to 2.0 liters as the main change for '87, and '88 brought a Cavalier-style "taillift" and an end to the soft top SE. A new instrument panel arrived for 1989.

Of all the GM divisions, only Olds ignored the ragtop renaissance. A shame, for a convertible Toronado might have been very appealing.

American Motors, briefly owned by Renault before being taken over by Chrysler in 1987, made a curious re-entry to the convertible ranks in 1985 via the front-drive subcompact Renault Alliance, with convertible conversion by ASC. The car actually put AMC in fourth place for the first time since the Sixties—in convertible sales, that is. A base price of just over $10,000 made the Alliance the least expensive ragtop in America—appealing to some despite a standard 1.4-liter four that was no road burner; an optional 1.7 was peppier. AMC sold 7143 soft top Alliances for 1985, but sales dwindled to 1651 a year later, as Japanese competitors made their presence known.

Still pushing water uphill, AMC came back for '87 with "pocket rocket" GTA models: a $9000 two-door sedan and a $13,000 convertible. A new 95-bhp 2.0-liter four delivered 0-60 in under 10 seconds, and an uprated suspension provided near sports-car cornering power (though claimed lateral acceleration was optimistic at 0.89g). But the GTA was the first thing to go following the Chrysler buyout.

Two small independent automakers offered convertibles during the decade: Avanti and Excalibur. Avanti's appeared for 1987, sporting a 305-cid Chevy V-8 producing 185 bhp or, optionally, 205. Handcrafted with a fiber-

glass body, the Avanti convertible was priced at about $40,000, a sum that jumped considerably before the end of the decade. Production figures are unavailable for 1987; the apparent sales high point came in 1989, when 151 of the ragtops were sold.

Excalibur first appeared in 1964, fashioning itself after the 1928 Mercedes SSK two-seat roadster. True Excalibur convertibles did not appear until 1980 (with roll-up windows), and while the two models continued to be called "Roadster" and "Phaeton," they were more accurately convertible coupes. By the late Seventies, Excaliburs were powered by Chevy small-blocks (350/305). Prices that hovered around $38,000 in 1980 had escalated to about $72,000 by the end of the decade. The number of Excaliburs built during those years varied annually, rarely exceeding 300 as a combined total. Excalibur struggled on through the Eighties but by 1990 had filed for Chapter 11.

While some of the convertibles introduced in the Eighties would not live to see 1990, the revival as a whole must be considered a resounding success. Much of this can be attributed to the advent of outside specialty firms capable of performing the conversions, thereby freeing the manufacturers from prohibitive investments of time, money, and assembly space.

At the close of the decade, there were no fewer than eight convertibles being offered by the Big Three—most through GM. Although still a very small percentage of total industry volume, production exceeded 150,000 units for 1989, enough to ensure the breed's survival into the Nineties.

Chapter 7: 1990-1994
The Fun Continues

Convertibles roll on in the Nineties sportier and more enticing than ever. The hard-to-resist beauty seen here is a 1994 Chevrolet Camaro Z28.

All of the convertibles available from the Big Three in 1989 carried over into the Nineties, except one. Despite a strong third-place showing on the sales charts in the late Eighties, the Chevy Cavalier convertible was dropped at the end of 1989. Because the Beretta ragtop that was to replace it was delayed by conversion problems, Chevy entered the 1990 model year with just the Corvette and two Camaro convertibles—three cars with a combined volume only slightly higher than that of the lone Cavalier model.

Corvette began the new decade with a revised instrument panel and driver-side air bag for 1990; rectangular taillamps (à la the ZR-1) followed for 1991. A more robust base engine arrived for '92, the 5.7 LT1 V-8, rated at 300 horsepower. Also, a new traction control system, Acceleration Slip Regulation (ASR), became standard on all 'Vettes for '92. Torque was tweaked slightly on the base engine for 1993, and horsepower of the ZR-1's mighty 5.7-liter V-8 rose by 30, to 405. That same model year brought a 40th Anniversary Ruby Red trim option, available on all Corvettes.

For 1994, the price of a Corvette convertible rose $1765, to $42,960. Convertibles gained a heated glass backlight and all 'Vettes got a passenger-side air bag. Although very expensive, a Corvette ragtop remained one of the most exciting ways to fly.

The big news for the 1990 Camaro was a driver-side air bag, and a 3.1-liter V-6 to replace the 2.8 as the standard

Left row, above, from top: Buick's pretty but doomed 1990 Reatta; 1990 Geo Metro, built by Suzuki and sold by Chevy dealers; 1990 Ford Mustang GT convertible, with 5.0-liter V-8 rated at 225 bhp. *Top:* The proposed but as yet unseen Chevy Beretta convertible (*foreground*), with 1990 Indy pace car counterpart. *Above center:* Pontiac's $13,934 Sunbird LE convertible for 1990. *Above right:* The 1990 Oldsmobile Cutlass Supreme listed for $20,995; only 464 were built.

engine on the Camaro RS. Chevy dropped its sponsorship of the International Race of Champions before the 1991 model year, and thus replaced the Camaro IROC badging with the reintroduced Z28 logo for that season. A "Heritage Appearance" option celebrating Camaro's 25th Anniversary was offered for '92.

A bold inside-and-out Camaro redesign for 1993 brought swoopy new styling, standard dual air bags and anti-lock brakes, and a new top engine: a detuned, 275-bhp version of Corvette's 300-horse 5.7 V-8 (ditto for the similar Pontiac Firebird Formula and Trans Am models). Base Camaros, powered by a 3.4-liter 160-bhp V-6, lost the RS designation. The evolutionary changes were welcome, but there was one sore point: New-design Camaro and Firebird convertibles were not available until the 1994 model year.

More Chevy convertible news came from Cavalier, which reintroduced a ragtop model for 1992, when plans for the aforementioned Beretta convertible were put on the back burner. Available in RS or sportier Z24 trim for

Top row, from left: Cadillac's 1991 Allanté came in at $61,450 with optional hardtop; '91 Chevy Camaro Z28 convertible had 245 horses. *Second row, from left:* 1991 Chevy Corvette convertible cost $38,770; the popular '91 Chrysler LeBaron. *Third row, from left:* 1991 Dodge Shadow ES ragtop started at $14,068; '91 Ford Mustang GT. *Far left:* The Aussie-made, Mercury-marketed '91 Capri. *Left:* Swoopy Pontiac Firebird for 1991.

'92 and '93, the Cavalier convertible offered a 2.2-liter 110 bhp four as the standard engine for the RS; optional on RS and standard on the Z24 was a 3.1-liter 140 bhp six. The 2.2 was slightly tweaked for '94.

At Pontiac, the Sunbird convertible saw minor alterations for 1990 and a more significant addition for '91: a 3.1-liter V-6 to replace the turbo four. Anti-lock brakes became standard for 1992. Changes were minor for 1993 and '94, although the latter model year brought 15-inch wheels and tires for the convertible.

Cadillac's slow-selling Allanté gained two noteworthy features for 1990: a driver-side air bag and traction control. Following minor changes for 1991 and '92, 1993 brought good news . . . and bad. Allanté gained the world-class 4.6-liter Northstar V-8, a twin-cam 32-valve aluminum powerplant rated at 295 horsepower, 95 more than the 4.9-liter ohv eight it replaced. But the bad news was the worst possible: GM announced in 1993 that Allanté would be discontinued after the model year, a victim of sluggish sales. Always a car of great promise, Allanté was nonetheless plagued by build problems and a perceived lack of real prestige (this despite a 1993 price of $61,675). It is ironic that when most of the bugs were finally ironed out and the car received the engine it always deserved, GM gave up and pulled the plug.

Buick's return to the convertible market came in mid-1990, with the launch of a droptop version of the elegant, two-seat Reatta, which had bowed in 1988. The convertible version of this hand-built honey was converted by ASC, and sold for about $35,000—a serious piece of

Top row, from left: 1992 Cadillac Allanté Indianapolis 500 pace car; '92 Chevy Corvette convertible; '92 Chevy Cavalier RS ragtop. *Second row, from left:* 1992 Chevrolet Camaro Z28 convertible; '92 Chrysler LeBaron LX; '92 Ford Mustang LX convertible. *Bottom row, from left:* 1992 Mercury Capri; '92 Pontiac Sunbird; '92 Pontiac Firebird Trans Am convertible.

change for an admittedly pretty car that was neither outstandingly quick nor nimble. Power for coupe and droptop alike came from the corporate 165-bhp "3800" V-6. Five more horses were added for 1991, Reatta's final model year. But sales hardly improved from the approximately 8500 sold for 1990 (including about 2100 convertibles). Like Allanté, Reatta was unable to fill its perceived niche.

Oldsmobile entered the convertible fray for the first time since 1975 when it introduced a $20,995 ragtop rendition of its front-wheel-drive Cutlass Supreme in 1990. Standard engine for 1990 and '91 was a 3.1-liter 140 bhp V-6. The convertible was hefty at 3600 pounds (versus the 3200 pounds of its coupe sibling), so performance was "gentlemanly," at best. New styling front and rear arrived for '92, while 1993 gave buyers the option of a hot 3.4-liter 200 bhp V-6 (available with automatic transmission only). Handsome and reasonably quick with the 3.4, the Cutlass convertible was distinguished visually by a "targa bar," which was originally the car's B-pillar. Olds claimed the bar strengthened the car's body, but its more practical use was as an anchor for door handles and shoulder belts. Standard goodies for all '94 Cutlass Supremes included a

Top row, from left: 1993 Cadillac Allanté, the model's last hurrah; '93 Chevy Cavalier Z24; '93 Chrysler LeBaron GTC. *Second row, from left:* 1993 Chevrolet Corvette convertible; '93 Mercury Capri. *Above:* 1993 Ford Mustang LX 5.0-liter. *Far left:* 1993 Olds Cutlass Supreme. *Left:* '93 Pontiac Sunbird SE.

driver-side air bag, and leather seats became standard on the convertible.

At Chrysler, the LeBaron convertible—America's best-selling droptop—carried on into the Nineties with two new engines and transmissions: the Mitsubishi-built 3.0-liter V-6 and an intercooled 174-bhp 2.2; the latter could be teamed with a heavy-duty five-speed manual on the sporty GTC model. Oddly, the 2.2 was replaced by a beefed-up 2.5 152-bhp turbo for 1991. Anti-lock brakes became an option for 1992, and the 2.5 turbo was discontinued for '93, leaving a 141-bhp 3.0-liter six as the hottest engine. Dual air bags became standard on all '94 LeBarons.

As for the pricey, LeBaron-like TC, only minor changes were made for 1990, and production was halted late that year. Little wonder, for of the 7300 TCs that were produced in total, just 2924 were sold during the 1989 model year, 3997 in '90. The remainder were reserialed as 1991 models.

The TC debacle aside, Chrysler cannily moved downmarket with its next convertible, the ASC-converted 1991 Dodge Shadow that started at about $13,000. Because Shadow was the lowest-priced convertible in America, certain niceties were unavailable—including a power top.

Changes were slight for 1992, but anti-lock brakes were a new option for '93, by which time the most potent available engine was a Mitsubishi-built 3.0-liter 141-bhp V-6. The Shadow name continued for 1994, but the convertible was dropped. It should be noted that, although Shadow was built from the same design as the Plymouth Sundance, the latter make never offered a convertible.

And, no, we haven't overlooked the upmarket—and awesome—Dodge Viper that hit showrooms in 1992. But because it lacked roll-up side windows, it was not a true convertible, and thus is not explored in this book.

Unlike GM and Chrysler, Ford stuck with a single offering since rejoining the convertible market back in 1983. It's the Mustang, of course, based on a venerable platform that, age aside, continued to do well for Ford through the 1993 model year.

Air bags were added to all Mustangs for 1990, and '91 brought a twin-plug head to the 2.3-liter four, raising output from 88 bhp to 105. As before, convertibles were available in LX or sportier GT guise. By 1993, the most muscular engine was the 5.0-liter V-8, rated at 245 horsepower only for the limited-edition, midyear Cobra package; for the GT and uplevel LX, the 5.0 produced 205 bhp. A driver-side air bag was standard on all Mustangs.

The big news for Mustang fans was a redesign for the 1994 model year, including, of course, a convertible. Although an update of the existing platform instead of a completely new car, the '94 had an aggressively restyled body, a removable fiberglass hardtop (optional), and a new base engine: a 3.8-liter V-6 instead of the previous 2.3-liter four. The top engine, while still a 5.0-liter V-8, was new as well, a slight reworking of the Thunderbird eight; horsepower in the Mustang iteration was 215 (up from 200 in the T-bird), with 285 pounds/feet of torque. Also new for '94 were optional anti-lock brakes, ensuring that the still-galloping ponycar could be reined to a halt more safely than ever before.

As we approach mid-decade, then, the convertible appears healthy, even robust. This despite an ever-increasing price gap between convertibles and their less-expensive closed counterparts. This gap has widened not merely in real dollars but relatively; a 10 percent price differential was to be expected in the early Sixties, but 30 years later the gap could be as high as 65 percent. Clearly, convertibles have become more expensive over the years, and more the province of moneyed buyers.

Considering this price differential, it's surprising that today's convertibles sell as well as they do. Indeed, pres-

Opposite, clockwise from top left: 1994 Chevrolet Cavalier RS, long in the tooth but still going strong; '94 Chevy Corvette convertible, undoubtedly the most exciting American ragtop; the appealing '94 Olds Cutlass Supreme; '94 Mercury Capri (*foreground*) and Capri XR2. *Above:* The excitingly redesigned Mustang for 1994 offered the brute power of the GT (*foreground*), plus a new V-6 base model (*right*). The first-edition '65 Mustang is at left.

ent-day convertible production is at a level not seen since the late Sixties. Despite a federal-government decree that 1994 cars shall have dual passive restraints (which may kill off some "marginal" convertibles), the ragtop's future seems assured. In addition to the many purely domestic models discussed in this book, buyers can choose from among numerous imports (Mazda's Miata is a sterling example), as well as many "hybrid" droptops, such as the Australian-built Capri, which came to Mercury showrooms in 1991.

Enthusiasts of open-air motoring surely have a wealth of alternatives. And the future may bring more choices—perhaps the rumored Saturn or Cadillac Eldorado droptops, or the much-anticipated Plymouth Prowler. As long as buyer interest in convertibles continues, the essence of romance—automotive and otherwise—will be alive and well in America.

INDEX